Four Years Below Zero

Wilma M. Knox
With Robert G. Knox

Edited by S. Kara Naber
Research by Mark Andrews

The Tennyson Press
Post Office Box 1638
Deming, N. M. 88031

First edition,February 2016
Limited to 500 copies

Library of Congress Cataloguing-in-Publication Data
Knox, Wilma 1920 – 2015
ISBN: 978-0-578-17384-9
Autobiography

The Tennyson Press
P.O. Box 1638
Deming, NM 88031
USA

Printed in the United States of America
Signature Book Printing, www.sbpbooks.com

DEDICATION

This book is dedicated to the memory of my niece, Mildred Mae Saunders. Millie helped me greatly in getting my job on the Trans-Alaska Pipeline and provided me with much aid and comfort in all the years I spent working on the Arctic line. Millie also worked on the line and died of pneumonia on January 31, 1984 while working at Prudhoe Bay.

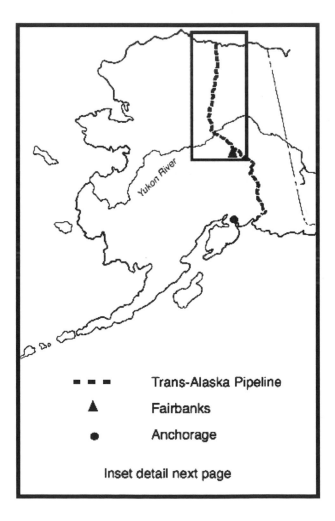

Trans-Alaska Pipeline
▲ Fairbanks
● Anchorage

Inset detail next page

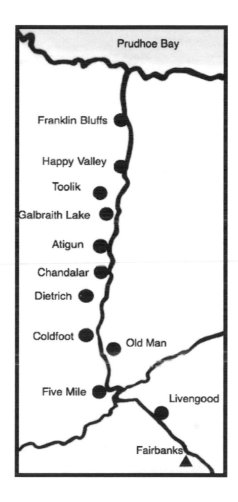

Wilma's chosen work area,
the Arctic section of the pipeline.

Contents

FOREWORD

As construction was just getting started in 1975 on the giant Trans-Alaska Pipeline Project, Wilma Knox was busy going around putting in her job applications with all of the firms involved. On those applications, Wilma described herself as a 55-year-old housewife and long-time Alaska resident. That was accurate as far as it went, but it told only a small part of her story.

We had arrived in the then Territory of Alaska in 1951 after driving north to Anchorage over the Alaska Highway. In the 24 years we lived in Alaska, we had both worked as writers and photographers and we spent all of our spare time traveling over the North by car, by plane, and many wilderness miles on foot. We had published a number of newspaper and magazine articles about those travels and wilderness camping. In 1973, a California publisher brought out our book about those experiences.

Wilma saw the go-ahead for construction of the 800-mile pipeline as a new opportunity and a challenge. In recent years, I had become overly busy editing a new monthly magazine and this had ended our chances for travel. Now Wilma saw the pipeline as possibly a new chance for her. A job on the line would give her the opportunity to build up our savings for the retirement years. But more than that, she saw it as a challenge for a woman to secure a job on this giant wilderness construction project. Women had never before had such a chance. And Wilma also saw it as another great adventure.

Wilma did get her job. She was one of more than a thousand women who went to work on the pipeline. An InteriorDepartment report in 1977 said that women made up almost 10 percent of all the craft workers on the job. But many of the jobs women took were for inside work in offices, barracks and messhalls. Many of these jobs were located in the larger "civilized camps" near Fairbanks and other communities on south to Valdez. Wilma's job was very different.

She went to work in March of 1975 for a security company operating in the far northern Arctic section of the line. This was the area where the U.S. record cold temperature of 80 below zero was recorded. Her job called for her to walk foot patrols around the camp areas all through the long, cold winters. It was indeed what she wanted: a chance to make high wages working 12 hours a day, seven days a week. And it *was* a new adventure and challenge to work outdoors in this harsh wilderness environment.

Unlike the majority of the women (and men) who signed up for pipeline jobs, Wilma stuck with her job all through the construction years, and she returned again to work in the Arctic when the pipeline started producing.

In many ways, it was a life-changing experience for her and one she wanted to remember and write about. All through the pipeline years, she had kept a day-by-day record in her journals. She also managed to find the time to write numerous letters to me and to her sister, Bette, about her experiences.

Later on, in her retirement years, she spent a lot of time gathering together all of this material and arranging it in manuscript form. Then she started writing what was to be a book about her years "on the job." But then, before she completed the final manuscript – at the age of 90 – she suffered a series of small strokes and lost her memory. She spent her last four years battling the effects of Alzheimer's Disease.

In all of the years since the pipeline was completed, there has been only a handful of books written about this giant construction job that ranked in size and scope with completion of the first U.S. transcontinental railroad or the digging of the Panama Canal. The pipeline played an important role in Alaska's 20th Century history, and there have been few books written by anyone who worked on the line during the construction years. And certainly none by or about a woman who worked the whole job – and in the Arctic.

That's why we feel this book is important enough to merit publication. It represents a very small but vital part of Alaska's 20th Century history. That is why, after Wilma's death in June of 2015, I started the job of putting the manuscript into final form. Two of our very good and long-time friends, Mark Andrews and Kara Naber, joined me in the project. Without their expert help, this book would never have appeared.

Robert G. Knox

Editor's comments

Despite her small stature, Wilma was a powerhouse. She was feisty, outspoken, opinionated, and determined but also extremely private.

After a 25-year acquaintance, I knew little about her work on the pipeline until we started working on this book. The details revealed in the text made me admire her more than I already did.

Long before it was popular, Wilma was a staunch feminist. Nothing riled her more than discrimination toward women. When faced with male chauvinism on the job, there must have been times when it was difficult for her to keep her cool. But there were other challenges as well; long hours, boring duty, emotional isolation, bitter cold and having to deal with drunks, druggers and grizzly bears. Sheer determination got her through the roughest and coldest of times.

The fact that she accepted all of these challenges, chose to work in the Arctic section (the most challenging location of all) and stayed as long as she did tells much more about her character than I could describe with words.

I feel sure that one of the reasons she took the job was to participate in the unique opportunity the pipeline afforded women and the chance to prove that women could not only do these jobs but do them well. She certainly did.

I'm grateful to have the opportunity to bring Wilma's pipeline experience to the public. It was a privilege to know her and to be counted as a friend.

S. Kara Naber

Researcher's comments

My wife, Kara and I first met Bob and Wilma Knox at a remote campground in central New Mexico called Datil Wells. We were working as campground hosts when Wilma and Bob arrived in a modest camper van. A friendship was formed that has lasted over 25 years.

Wilma was small of stature, with a pixie smile and a mind sharper than the finest Sheffield steel. She was a walker, a vegetarian, and protector of women's rights. Through the years, we learned about some of her views and achievements but little about her work on the pipeline until we helped Bob publish her recollections of that time.

What an adventure – the cold, the loneliness, the isolation and the challenge of the work!

In later years, as Wilma's health began to deteriorate, Bob promised to publish her memoirs, which he has done. To quote Robert Service, an old sourdough himself, "A promise made is a debt unpaid, and the trail has its own stern code."

Wilma passed in the summer of 2015. She is missed.

Mark Andrews

Heading for the Line

The Wien Airline F-27 prop-jet banked sharply as the pilot lined it up to land on the gravel runway. With my nose glued to the porthole window, I watched the landscape gliding by. In the distance, I could see the snowy peaks of the Brooks Range. Just below us were several rows of barracks-like buildings. In back of them there seemed to be a small lake and a winding stream. This was Galbraith Lake pipeline camp. The date was March 29, 1975, and this strange and remote place in Arctic Alaska was to be my home as well as my work-place for months to come.

That is, if I made the grade. It was sink or swim time for me.

My journey to this far-out spot had started a couple of days earlier in my hometown of Anchorage. There were late March splotches of snow on the ground at Anchorage's International Airport as we hurried into the terminal. The flight to Fairbanks was just about to depart, and we had to trot to the gate.

I was torn between intense excitement and intense sorrow as I hugged Bob, my husband of 27 years, good-bye.

"Write," he whispers in my ear, "Be sure to write as soon as you can. Or better, call!"

Tears came to my eyes and my throat was tight. Perhaps I shouldn't go. Bob looks careworn, lines of confusion and sadness in his face. Seeing them, my determination and excitement return. The reason for my going to the Pipeline is clear. I am determined to make enough money so we no longer have to live from payday to payday and so we will have a nest egg for the years ahead. Surely, one year should do it – or at least I hope so.

The flight is called and I must go. Bob folds me close, and then, turning, walks away down the hall. For a moment I am overwhelmed by the sight of his rusty black raincoat and his grey hair moving away, and too soon lost from view.

Nothing in my life will ever be the same again, but this, of course, I do not know.

THE FLIGHT NORTH was short, smooth and un-eventful. From where I sat, it appeared the 737 was pretty well full. It also appeared, from what I could see, that I was the only woman on the plane. My seat partner was a huge young man who had to squeeze into his seat to fit. He said that he works for Goodyear, has been in Anchorage for 16 years, but this is first trip as far as Fairbanks and he has made but one trip to Homer. (How sad.)

Once we land and walk into the terminal, we find it a scene of mad inactivity. The room is crowded with people (almost all men) with a wide variety of suitcases, duffel bags, toolboxes and what have you. The men and their luggage are standing, sitting, and lying on the floor and centered around the Alyeska booth. They are all just waiting to be called for a flight out to a pipeline camp.

I manage to elbow my way to the airport manager's office and get an okay to leave my bags while I go have coffee. It is only a little after 8:00 a.m. and much too early to go out to the NANA Security office.

I am already starting to feel some twinges of homesickness, but I manage to control them. I am very aware that for me this is *The Big Adventure!* I wouldn't trade places with anyone I know. I want to record every one of the sights, sounds, and thoughts in my new life. Right there in the cafeteria, I start on a daily journal.

It's a very colorful crowd – very few women. Some very young men and the bearded, long hair types with fancy hats, and the older, crusty ones who look like they have worked construction since their infancy. The background conversation seems to be about Tonsina, where the first pipe of the line will go in today.

GET MY BAGS and go down to catch a cab. It takes awhile, but I finally get one and go out to the NANA Security office. (This is the outfit which will actually be my employer on the pipeline. It's owned by the NANA Corporation, one of the regional corporations set up in the Native Claims Settlement Act.)

A young woman working in the office, Linda, introduces me to two young Native men, one from Shungnak, and the other from Kivilina, and another equally young guy from Massachusetts. We all fill out paperwork – this is a Laborers' Union job – for what seems like hours. Then we go into Captain Nix's office and he gives a long talk on what we can expect of the job and what not. He seems very nice.

Next, we are each issued clothing orders and we go back downtown to Carr's Men's Store and the Northern Commercial Company. Getting fitted for clothing was turned into something of a hassle for me by the heavy-handed, sexist humor from the store clerk. When I asked if they had sizes for women, I was told with a sly smile:

"Why, we don't believe in discrimination! We're *letting* you wear men's clothing. After all, you'll be filling men's jobs!"

I let that go by and concentrated on the clothes. They are all too big and I'll have to have them altered as soon as possible.

We did each get a beautiful $221 Arctic parka, down-filled with a wolf ruff, in a nice green. Mine is the smallest size available but so long it reaches midway between knees and ankles but damned cozy.

We also get grey woolen trousers and jacket (what the old-timers call the Alaska Tuxedo) and two cotton gray twill shirts that fit fairly well. All of the clothing cost – probably $350 so far – will be deducted gradually from our paychecks, along with Union dues, taxes, ad infinitum.

After the clothing business, I spent a couple of hours in town and had lunch. Then I started out to walk back to NANA. Along the way, I was adopted by an apparently lost police dog. I had to duck into a pizza parlor to shake him.

It takes me almost an hour of fast walking to get back to the office. I call my niece, Millie, and she comes down to pick me up, along with all of my gear. And it has bloomed into an awful lot. Millie has an Oregon woman friend over who is certainly interested in my job. (Since she is an ex-bartender, I fear for her chances with NANA.) We chat for a couple of hours and then go back downtown to pick up my trousers and a duffle bag for all the extra clothes. I must be up by 4:00 a.m. and out to Fort Wainwright Orientation Center by 6:00 a.m.

THE NEXT DAY, March 28, 1975, was probably the longest day of my life. Millie insisted on getting up early and taking me out to Wainwright. We had breakfast and I felt pretty well shot. I had hardly any sleep, what with the excitement about the job and much too much coffee. Later I would find out that most people going this route experience much the same thing.

At the center I found about 150 people – almost all men – getting their orientation. We were divided into three groups and spent the morning seeing slide shows, and getting lectures, about the Environment, Safety, Human Relations, Wildlife, Arctic Survival in Alaska, and the Camps. Then each group was taken into Fairbanks and everyone got a complete physical, including an EKG. I came out fine but was told that I need glasses, which I already knew.

Then it was back to the Center where we had lunch (all meals are free) and finished up with the lectures and slide shows by 2:15. A bus was taking us to the airport at 3:00 p.m. So I had 45 minutes to rush out and buy some boots. All the directors and instructors had warned us that we must have such boots and long underwear and insulated pants to get on the plane to fly out to camp. I bought boots two sizes too large (Sorel shoe pacs). I hate them and will try to get Bob to find some the right size. Or will wait until R & R. Anyway it was all hogwash about needing this stuff to get on the plane. No one gave a damn.

At the airport, we stow my gear by Gate 5 where pipeline workers go out. By now my shoulders are cut to the bone from carrying so much. It's murder! What a sight there at the gate – all those bearded men and stacks and stacks of gear, duffle bags and suitcases. There were just a few women in the crowd. Most of them sort of cruddy like myself by now. I sat in the cafeteria with a young Indian girl from Petersburg. She is going to Happy Valley. I also meet the girl's mother who is with the Equal Employment Opportunity office. Also a tall, black bearded lawyer from Ohio. I also spot my two Eskimo friends from NANA and the boy from New England.

Until 6:30 when we are scheduled to board, we just all sit on luggage, sometimes chatting and looking, but mostly waiting. Two odd-looking women arrive with their luggage. The Indian girl says they are a couple of hookers from downtown Fairbanks. (I didn't ask her how she knew, but just accepted the info matter-of-factly.) We are fascinated how they will get on the plane since, supposedly, all passengers must be employed on the pipeline, but they do get on. The smaller one is on our plane. She has a camera with at least a 600mm lens. The taller one was most interesting – a fur-trimmed, baby-blue coat just long enough to cover her crotch. And long legs in nylons – oh, very, very long legs. Hair beehived. I didn't see which plane she got on.

Chapter 1

WE EMBARK just about on time. One of the old F-27s. Galbraith is the first stop. All the others are on north. Galbraith is located 150 miles north of the Arctic Circle but still 140 miles south of Prudhoe. It is kind of a rough trip. The weather is none too good and the ride is quite bumpy. I sit next to a young mechanic who is also going to Galbraith. We chat all the way. He will be a fuel truck driver. As we are coming in I get a good view of part of the Brooks Range – a beautiful sight. Long, wide valleys and tall peaks. We drop lower and I can see the camp situated in a wide valley.

Once we land and I get off the plane, I find Sergeant Ray Causton of NANA waiting for me. He gives me the choice of starting to work immediately or waiting and sleeping until midnight. I take going to work at once. We go to the office and then to the barracks, where I meet my roommate, Jean Layman, a nice young woman from Fairbanks who has been working as a nurse for the past nine years.

I also meet the two men who will be working at night with me. One is Eric Sutcliffe, a young red-headed man, who has been working at Mount McKinley Park. He tells me he has bought land at Unalaska and built a house there. After the pipeline he plans to live there and work as a crab fisherman. The other man on the night shift is Gabriel (with a last name too difficult to remember) a young Eskimo from Nome.

I SPENT THAT FIRST NIGHT going the rounds with the Sergeant and learning what all I had to do. I am going to skip the details for now, but just say that it was an ordeal. I was exhausted, and when I finally got to sit down, I almost fell out of my chair. Naturally, I was not too alert and all the details of the camp layout were too confusing for my fuzzy-headedness.

At 6:00 a.m., when I got off shift, I went to my room, took a shower, and crawled into bed. The building is not really noisy. There are many day-sleepers, so there are "Quiet" signs posted on doors. I sleep well and awake at 3:00 p.m. feeling refreshed. That means I have three hours before I go to work again.

The buildings I am patrolling are just part of Camp Galbraith. The camp's population runs between 400 and 500 workers. Of that total some 20 to 30 are women. The barracks are 56-person and smaller. Both men and women are in the same ones but, of course, there are some – many – with only men. The newer barracks are very nice with carpeted floors: I am in one of these. There are large, immaculate restrooms and shower rooms and laundries, one set for the women on one side, another for men on the other.

The rooms for two people are small but attractive, with single beds, small desk and wardrobe arranged on either side – sparse but adequate. Everything everywhere is spic and span. Huge heaps of neatly folded towels and washrags in restrooms and showers. Beds are freshly made up each day. We cannot lock the room, but we can have a padlock to lock the wardrobe.

Once I got up, got dressed, and put myself together, I headed over to the messhall for a meal (supper or breakfast?) before reporting for work. The messhall itself is a large and very clean cafeteria. A small, outer room has a coffee urn and one with hot water for tea and cocoa. In the big refrigerator is juice, soda pop, ice cream bars, and pastries, brownies and other goodies. There is cream, honey, and sugar for drinks. There are also boxes of choice apples, oranges and sometimes pears and grapes. Help yourself. This room is open 24 hours and nothing ever runs out. It is called the "mug-up" room.

In the main dining room, where regular meals are served, the long tables hold condiments in a huge variety. The food is served cafeteria style with a salad bar and the salads are choice. There are hot dishes of all kinds along the serving line. That first night I had beef stroganoff. Then come pies, cakes and you name it. The food is very good and well prepared and cooked, and as much as you can hold.

After my meal, I made a quick walking tour of nearby buildings, just to get acquainted. I found there were recreational halls all over the place with pool tables, TV, and various games. There is a "library" with paper-backs and some magazines. A small concession, The Commissary, sells essentials: shaving supplies, padlocks, and so forth. I didn't have time to investigate everything, but I did find later that we have individual mail slots at the NANA office for any letters we might get. There is also a place there where I can store the camera and gadget bag.

Time was getting on, so I hurried back to my room, picked up my gear, and headed back to the office to check in. This would be my first full night of being on patrol alone.

I Was Not a Boy

I will admit that first night's work was hard. Very hard. That twelve-hour shift – working in the dark hours – took a lot of getting used to, but I was determined to make the grade if humanly possible. I wasn't afraid of hard work or long hours. My many years in Alaska, and a lot of time spent outdoors, had hardened me to the cold and darkness of winter. I knew it probably was going to be a long grind getting into the groove, but it certainly seemed to be doable.

Long hours and hard work had started early in my life. I was born and grew up on my parent's farm (or ranch, as the locals called it) in eastern Washington state, in the foothills of the Cascade Mountains. We were just a little way south of the Canadian border and part of a loose-knit farming community known as Pine Creek. The nearest actual town, Tonasket, with about a thousand residents, was some 17 miles away and reached – in dry weather – over dirt roads. My mother and father were true pioneers in the area.

My father had homesteaded the land, which was the basis for the ranch, and he gradually added to it over the years by buying up the nearby land of farmers who failed to make a go of it in that rugged land. William Didra was his name. He had staked the homestead when it was still a wilderness and built a barn and a log cabin, probably in that order. My mother, Cricket Gatewood, came along years later. She had been married before and had several almost-grown children. By the time they met and married, both were well into middle age but still they produced another family.

I know that my father was hoping for a son, or sons, to help him run the ranch and shoulder some of the variety of chores that had to be accomplished seven days a week to keep things going. What he got were two girls, me and my sister Bette, born three years later.

WHILE I WAS NOT THE BOY my father and mother had hoped for, I filled a boy's place in many ways around the ranch, thus removing a load from my parents' shoulders in at least a modest way. One task was to drive the milk cow herd to pasture in the morning and bring it back in late afternoon. One pasture was the Lemanoski Lake place two and a half miles away. Any transfer of stock – pigs, cattle or sheep – from one pasture to another in summer or on weekends during the school term, usually required my help. One of my tasks each spring was to ride to my mother's old homestead several miles on past our Oakes school after classes and pen our flock of sheep; then ride back in the morning to let them back out. The reason for keeping the sheep so far away from the home place was because in spring and early summer, grass was more advanced in this open country.

The ride to the now-deserted homestead involved an extra roundtrip of three miles each time, which meant going to school early and getting home late. But I liked the responsibility and the particular delights it held.

My mother's old homestead house was still standing, as well as other little buildings, such as an outhouse,

11

chicken house, and so on. Deserted as it was, I found it pleasantly eerie, especially in contrast with the sheep who were very much alive and real.

Sometimes I would sit on the hillside overlooking the old building and imagine how it must have been when my mother and her five children lived here. I could see my mother in a long dark skirt, with her sturdy figure and dark hair, singing as she went to feed her chickens. How young she must have looked then. But there was little time for day-dreaming, and with the sheep spread out across the hillside, I mounted my horse and we set out for school.

On such a bright spring morning, the meadow larks would be trilling their lovely short song. It all gave me a feeling of unbounded happiness.

But there was little time for sight-seeing or day-dreaming. After school other chores awaited us. Between the house and the spring that supplied us water, my mother maintained a huge and varied vegetable garden. It was an organic garden although we didn't know it at the time. Chemical fertilizers and plant additives were relatively unknown, and if they had been available, there was certainly no money to buy them. The various farm animals supplied the fertilizer, the spring supplied irrigation water, and my younger sister and I supplied much of the labor involved in hoeing, weeding and gathering the crops.

This was our busy, busy life growing up. There was hard work, and we spent our nights in a never-finished house with no electricity and no running water. There never seemed to be enough time or money to get the job finished. It may have been a hard life, but my sister and I were happy children. Even with school and all the chores we usually found some time for fun and games. This lasted until I was a teenager.

THEN IT ALL CAME TO a sudden end. There were two events that caused my world to collapse. First came the depression, then my father was taken seriously ill.

To start with, the national depression wasn't something we knew much about. There was no television in those days, and with no electricity in the house, we had no radio. The nearest town and newspaper were seventeen dusty miles away. Then came the Bank Holiday and the bank in Tonasket failed to open again. All of my father's capital and savings were in that bank. Suddenly, he was a man with a fair amount of land but hardly a dollar to his name.

It wasn't long after this that my father became ill. After several trips to town and one long trip to the nearest city, we got the word. He had been diagnosed as having diabetes. Even today, it is a serious and even deadly disease. Back then it was a death sentence. He failed rapidly. I don't know if the disease, combined with the loss of all his savings was the cause, but he seemed to lose the will to live.

After his death, events moved rapidly. Within what seemed only a few months, my mother was married again to a nearby rancher. Taking Bette with her, she moved into her new home. I was left behind to mind what was left of the ranch, but only until an auction was held and the ranch sold. Then I was really cast adrift.

Mom apparently had no room in her new home for a 17-year-old daughter, and I was shifted about for visits – some brief and some longer – with one half-sister and another. I tried to find work, but with the exception of a brief stint in a vegetable packing plant, there was just nothing in this poor, rural area for a female high school graduate. Finally, I took the one path that was open: The result was a brief, failed marriage to a local cowboy.

Then Mom took pity on me. She deeded over to me a small piece of land she retained from her homestead. That turned out to be my ticket to freedom.

I was able to sell the land, and with a few hundred dollars in hand, I set out on the first leg of the very long journey that brought me here to Arctic Alaska.

Along with another girl from the area who wanted to go to college, and some $300 in cash, I arrived in Los Angeles looking for a job and wanting to go to school. I was very lucky with the job: I was hired by an older woman who ran a small plant manufacturing lamp-shades and who needed a general office gofer. That job lasted all the time I went to college.

The college course seemed a long, hard slog at the time, but I did end up with two things that really determined my future and set the stage for all of the adventures in the years ahead. I graduated with a degree in Journalism, and in the Journalism classes I met Bob, my future husband.

Less than a year after my graduation, Bob was working in the small city of Rock Springs, Wyoming,

14

first as a reporter and then managing editor of two newspapers, the *Daily Rocket* and the *Sunday Miner.* I joined him there and on June 9, 1949 we were married in the nearby county seat of Green River, Wyoming. From the very first, we both determined to move north to Alaska. Bob started a letter-writing campaign to publications in the territory and when that failed to bring on immediate results we moved at least north to Yakima, Washington where he had been offered a job as the world news editor for a larger newspaper, *The Yakima Republic.*

That didn't last long, just a few months. Norman C.Brown, publisher of the *Anchorage Daily News,* wrote Bob offering him a job as a reporter. At last! We were off in our old, secondhand Chevrolet coupe traveling north over the long, dusty Alaska Highway to the 24 years of exploring the Far North that finally brought me here to this new adventure working in the Arctic.

NOW IT IS MARCH 30, 1975 – Easter Sunday. I saw the very beginning of Easter, believe me. Yesterday was snowy here – it just drifted down to a depth of about two inches or less. The temperatures are mild, perhaps as low as +20 and up to freezing. The air is crisp and fresh. By the way, our room has a window that opens, which is a blessing. It can be cool and good for sleeping, but I sure do wonder about the mosquito situation later. There are screens on the windows and since the doors are kept shut, it might not be bad.

I learned today that my roommate Jean is going on R & R in seven days. I have talked to some people here who have been here up to 13 weeks with no break. I feel I might not be able to stand it.

Everyone says time goes fast. No one has or even wants spare time, but I am determined to adjust my life to where I have some – as much as possible – for writing, reading, walking. I walk 8 to10 miles on my 12-hour shift, but it bothers me far less than it does most people. I am going to meditate both morning and afternoon faithfully, and hope to get my sleeping in seven hours. Can it be done? I'll know later.

On my shift from 6:00 p.m. to 6:00 a.m. I do a lot of walking and some riding on patrol. Perhaps in a few days I will drive the pickup myself once I learn the locations and directions.

I had a bit of a problem the first time in the company pickup. I will add here that I am no novice at pickup driving. I've driven the Alaska Highway in both directions by myself when we got new vehicles in Seattle and Bob was unable to make the trip. I was telling all this to Eric while we were driving out to the dynamite storage location, and he needled me into taking over the wheel. I did, and right away I put us over a little bank into deep snow. We were firmly stuck and finally Eric had to hitch back to camp and get another vehicle to pull us out.

Feeling that Eric secretly felt I was incompetent, a mere helpless woman, and older to boot, I was humiliated to the very marrow by this small accident, but I managed to hold back tears of rage and frustration, and vowed to myself it would never happen again. It never did!

I am sure that the night job will be optional before long, but I am – surprisingly – thinking I might like to keep it, at least for the summer. It will be interesting in the long, light nights. There will also be chances to see wildlife. I think too, that I am more on my own than days would permit.

There is even one other advantage: Since more work is done in the daytime, the barracks are fairly quiet at that time. Adding to the peace and quiet for me is that we have one day and one night shift worker in our room, so each has a maximum of privacy. All of my spare time is spent alone, which is good for writing. But this is not so good for Jean, who I know had wanted a roommate she could talk to. As it is, we mostly just get to say, "Hi!" as we come and go.

So really, all in all, I haven't minded working at night. Thus far I have been treated well, and the men I encountered have been nice. I will be extremely wary about being even normally friendly, however.

Now it's going on 5:00 p.m. and I must go and get Easter Dinner (or breakfast?) and put on my clothes for going to work. No lateness tolerated. We were warned this is just like jail. It is.

YOU REALLY DO SORT OF lose track of time in a life like this. It is very true that, with such hours, what day it is or what time of day, means very little. Now it is Monday, April 1, and I had to look at the calendar to check that out. I went to bed this morning at 8:00 a.m. on April 1 and now I have just had coffee and it is "morning" though really 3:30 in the afternoon. At 5:00 p.m. I will go over for breakfast – steaks?

My Thought For The Day: Being here at Galbraith is like living in the bottom of a white teacup – a deep,

deep teacup with a white lid. Everything is white and turns up. There is no horizon – the sky is white. The glare on a day like today is unbelievable. The camp itself is white on the outside – all of the buildings. Today there is a sharp breeze and it is semi-sunny, the sky is overcast with a thin haze. Ice crystals are falling. It all contributes to the overall whiteness. The air is dry. I have trouble with my nose and mouth drying out. One man in our outfit is going to bring back a small vaporizer when he goes on R & R. Perhaps I will too – in eight or so weeks that is!

But I can't complain. I am already beginning to adjust and feel less tired. The miles of walking are great – I'll soon be hard as nails.

Last night I did nothing but tour the barracks, both inhabited and the empty ones. It was very eerie walking through those empty ones – my footsteps echoed like something out of a Fright Movie. These are long, 56-man barracks. An arctic walkway connects them. It is not finished, so I could see the mountains and snowy landscape as it got light about 5:00 a.m. When the walkway is done, there will be no way to see out – no windows, but I enjoyed the crisp cold air as I came out of the hot barracks. (They keep the thermostats turned way up in all the buildings – like 80 degrees – because there isn't enough insulation in these prefabs for the Arctic. That's one reason we Guards have to keep checking the many, many furnaces in the camp – the danger of fire.)

Speaking of the barracks, even as I write this, the big cranes are all busy grabbing barracks sections off trailer trucks and swinging them into position to be bolted together. The camp is growing steadily. Apparently, it may get up to 1,000 or 1,200 people. I have also been told the amazing fact that Prudhoe is now the third largest city in Alaska!

I am still keeping up the journal that I started in the airport in Fairbanks, and I want to jot down facts like those.

Another fact that I learned about Prudhoe is that the place was named by the British explorer John Franklin way back in 1826. That seems rather amusing because most of us living in Alaska never heard of the name until the oil exploration in recent years. Lake Galbraith, on the other hand only got its name in 1951 to honor a bush pilot, Bart Galbraith, who was lost while flying in this area. I want to add facts like these, as there just is not enough about work – and some days are so dull – to fill up a journal. Of course, there is a good bit to write about as to the camp itself, the various people, and so on.

By the way, some of the people hold us security guards in scorn, but for the most part, we are regarded with good-natured tolerance by just about everyone else. I am known as "The Secret Service."

Here's a couple of the most recent jottings in my journal just to give you an idea of what I am trying to put down and remember:

> April 19. Eric spotted the first songbird. Temperature about 6 above. We also saw a land otter and den on the river. Found tracks (turned out to be parky squirrels).

April 20. Warm and sunny. Melting. Ate breakfast and got to bed late (first time). Walked out of camp and found patches of bare ground with mosses and lichens. Some photos. Really nice out. Too warm in room. Jean Layman came back from R & R. Walked 9 miles through barracks (according to my pedometer).

April 21. Partly sunny. Not so warm. Received a "Hero" medal from Lt. Big surprise. Somewhat embarrassed. Found blisters are forming on heels. Very active evening – Dennis and I had two false fire alarms. Went to Medic and got big jar of lanolin ointment to rub on feet. It really helps when I have to walk as many as 15 miles a night.

There it is. That's the kind of stuff I have been putting down in my journal. It's nothing real exciting but just the daily events as I remember them. I don't expect anyone else will ever read it, but it will help to jog my memories of these days.

Chapter 3

The Camps

During my early days at Galbraith, I was able to get really oriented and form a clear picture in my mind of the layout of the camp due to a happy circumstance. While making my rounds one evening, I stopped to talk with a man sitting in the rec room who, for some reason, looked familiar. He told me he was a helicopter pilot and then I remembered that some years before, he, Bob and I had been marooned together for a couple of days in the old "hotel" at Point Barrow. The hotel wasn't much, but at least we were snug and warm while a fierce winter-like storm raged outside.

Now, while we were chatting, the pilot mentioned that he would be making a brief flight around the area the next morning. "Would you like to go along?" he asked. Since I would be off duty then, I jumped at the chance.

From the air, the camp seemed incredibly small – just one cluster of assorted buildings huddled together in an endless, overwhelming outback. It was one little civilized spot situated next to the winding, gravel Haul Road.

While my brief aerial view was of just one camp, I would learn in days to come that the all of the construction camps north of the Yukon River and on into the Arctic looked pretty much the same. In due time, I would visit, however briefly, all eleven of these NANA-policed camps: Five Mile, Old Man, Prospect, Cold Foot, Dietrich, Chandalar, Atigun, Galbraith, Toolik, Happy Valley, and Franklin Bluffs. Some were bigger, some

21

smaller but, regardless of size, they all consisted of the same look-alike buildings. Then, in between the construction camps, were four nearly-completed pump station installations: Pump Stations One, Three, Four, and Five. These would remain and be in operation along with the oilfield community of Prudhoe Bay on the Arctic Ocean and at the northern end (or beginning) of the pipeline.

Then, when the oil started flowing south in the pipeline, all of our construction camps would be closed and the buildings hauled away or torn down.

All of the northern camps (but not the pump stations) were nearly identical in layout. Each consisted of modular unit living quarters, messhall and kitchen, offices, radio room, mechanics' shops, firehouse, sewage treatment plant, water treatment plant, warehouse complex, craft shop area, paint and tire shops, battery shop, airport, heliport, gas pump, and POL where huge amounts of fuel was stored, and a large area of open storage for all sorts of supplies from machine parts to lumber.

The buildings were pretty much laid out according to the same plans at each camp, and by no means simply helter skelter. After camp sites were selected, the area was cleared and leveled and, if needed, gravel pads were laid down. Shops, warehouses, water and sewage treatment, generator housing and the like were loosely clustered, the POL was put off to one side by itself, while barracks, offices, messhall, theater and radio room were arranged in another section.

Each camp was really a small and isolated but self-sufficient town. Each was complete with underground and/or utilidor lines, designated parking areas (with no meters), streets and street lighting, fire department, movie houses, store, cafeteria, offices, homes, gyms, and post office.

The barracks came in several different varieties. There were the 20-person units with central showers, toilets, and laundry facilities for each; 56-person units with separate facilities for men and women; and 52-person units, which were often the nicest and very similar to the 56-person units. In camps where I worked, the 52-person units were generally the newest and nicest and, almost always, one of these was designated as a so-called "women's barracks." An exception to this was at our southern-most camp, Five Mile, where the women had been shunted aside to some old, oddball units that looked as if they had been thrown together and now were all but falling apart.

Fifty-two and 56-person units were manufactured in sections that were easy to transport, one each on a flat-bed truck. There were eight of these sections to a unit. Once on location, the sections were lifted by large cranes onto heavy timber foundations already in place, with door ends facing across hallways. Roofs and floors were then installed over and under hallways; sections firmly bolted together; electrical and plumbing lines connected to the camp's system, and in a matter of little more than hours, an entire small town was ready for occupancy.

I never did see any of the 20-person units being moved; most of them were at the camp sites from the very beginning, some from the oil exploration days; and at least at Happy Valley, many of these units were hardly usable by the time of actual pipeline construction. When very cold weather arrived, these small, separate units bore the brunt of high winds and often had to be vacated because the plumbing froze. At Happy, Barracks A through H – collectively know as "the Ghetto"– were small house-like structures clustered on a hillside.

Often the larger units were arranged in double rows, end to end, with heated arctic walkways built between the units. These walkways, with a plywood roof, floor and walls, made it possible to carry on a great many activities without ever being exposed to the weather.

For instance, if you lived in Happy Valley B Camp, once you arrived home from work, you walked into a heated, wide hallway that led to your barracks. You showered, changed clothes, and went to the messhall in your shirtsleeves and carpet slippers to have dinner. Afterward, you could go to the post office to pick up mail, to the theater for a free movie, or to the rec room to shoot pool or play any of the other games. Possibly you continued down the hall to visit the medic; to go to the commissary to pick up a new magazine; to the Mug Up room for fresh coffee, pastry or fruit; then back to your room to hit the sack (or to a friend's room for a nightcap). The Arctic winds, snow and cold were often raging outside, but the rooms were comfortable and the walkway reasonably warm.

Unfortunately, not all the camps were so conveniently arranged. In some others, portions were built with walkways but not all living quarters were in one unit. For instance, just across the road, in Happy's A Camp, the messhall was separate from most of the barracks. So a mad dash through the cold was a prelude to meals for everybody except the lucky few who happened to live in the four dorms connected to the messhall.

FOR WHATEVER REASON – economy or quality, or both – nearly all the living and office units were Canadian built by a Calgary-based firm named ATCO. That was a hard name not to see, and everyone who worked on the pipeline will probably always remember it. The units were all white aluminum sided. Each had a band of orange-yellow around the top and in big, black letters the name ATCO.

Those trailer sections were transported to the camps by truck with all the furnishings inside, even the beds, blankets, and linens. Once the sections were bolted together, bullcooks washed down dusty or muddy walls along the hallway. Black, rubber runners were then unrolled the length of the hallways in the 56-person units (the 52-person units were carpeted) to cushion footsteps and make the building more quiet, as well as for the sake of appearance.

SELDOM IN THE HISTORY OF MANKIND, and certainly never before in the far North, had workers on any construction project lived so luxuriously on the job. All the rooms in the units were carpeted. The rooms were small, just large enough to accommodate two single beds, two skimpy wardrobes, and two small dressers (doubling as writing desks) each with a mirror and chair.

Walls were attractively paneled in wood, with drapes in bright fabric. Desks and wardrobes were buff with black trim, and looked harmonious with the carpeting patterned in orange, yellow, black, and white. Bathrooms, located centrally near laundry rooms, were brightly lighted, with long rows of sinks and mirrors. Showers and toilets were often in separate rooms.

Each barracks was heated by four or eight furnaces (two in the little 20-man units), which were oil-fired with built-in humidifiers. If the furnaces and vents were carefully adjusted and never tampered with, rooms and hallways were normally comfortable, for they were designed to provide efficient air-conditioning.

Unfortunately, however, most thermostats were not lockable and accessible to everyone, as were the air vents. With such a wide diversity of occupants, the systems were more often than not working far below efficiency level, with numerous people from warmer climates attempting to set comfortable temperatures for themselves after days of working in bone-chilling cold. Once winter set in, a tug-of-war began between cold-blooded and warm-blooded occupants.

One roommate, who I had for a short time, worked on the same shift that I did. She nearly roasted me in those few short weeks. She not only opened all the heat vents so that the room temperature soared to 85 degrees or more, but she kept it like that all night and slept under four heavy blankets as well!

This was not at all unusual. In my opinion, all of the rooms were kept far too warm for comfort and certainly too warm for health. The Cheechakos were overcompensating for the extreme cold outside, and the rest of us had to go along.

Arctic cold is unbelievably dry, and the effect is compounded by furnace heat. The furnace humidifiers were totally inadequate. Separate humidifiers were provided for some rooms and offices. Some residents used rolls of toilet tissue or paper towels, placing them in containers of water where they acted as wicks to throw off moisture in the air. My second year on the job, I bought a $15 humidifier, which shot a fine stream of water into the air while I slept. It provided a more refreshing sleep and, in the end, cured my cold problem.

HUMIDIFIERS WERE JUST ONE example of the dozens of innovations residents employed to make their camp rooms more comfortable or pleasant. The pleasant diversion of changing your room around or "fixing it up" was introduced to me almost on the day of my arrival in camp. It was really a game, a fad, a hobby, a contest, for people starved for creative activities. For the most part, camp life was unnatural and sterile. Among people who were reasonably certain of being in camp for at least one entire tour of nine weeks; for culinary and others who returned to the same camp tour after tour for sometimes years, a few actually built miniature homes around themselves.

Looking back on this odd obsession to "fix up," it does seem strange but still reasonable to someone who was there. No doubt it was a strong urge to remain an individual in difficult circumstances. In its less extreme form, it provided residents a relatively harmless pastime. Put succinctly, the man or woman engaged in redecorating simply did not have time or interest to be troublesome–at least until the project was finished and serious partying began for the purpose of showing off the results!

When fixing up was carried to excess by a large number of residents in all the camps – as it certainly must have been if my observations were correct – there is every chance that it cost Alyeska some serious money.

The loss was not in cost of materials used as much as it was in loss of man hours of skilled craftsmen. In the camps where I worked there were maintenance crews that included carpenters, plumbers, electricians, and often painters. These crews were kept busy at all times. Building of one sort or another continued right up until the last carpenter was let go.

This odd fact lent these very temporary wilderness cities a curious air of permanence, and their inhabitants the comfortable feeling that these wonderful jobs – and all this wonderful money – would go on and on forever.

That comfortable feeling was often expressed in such thoughts as: "Would Alyeska be building that porch at this nth hour if the job was about to fold up or would they be having those steps repaired so carefully? Of course not!"

An equally odd fact was that quite often camp residents seemed to believe that the craft people were there for the sole purpose of helping the residents to re-model their rooms. This was especially true of the carpenters, who were burdened with a great deal of this sub rosa work. The amount, variety, and quality of remodeling furniture that came out of line carpenters' shops north of the Yukon was staggering.

Smaller items such as shelves and shallow cabinets for tapes were among the more common pieces; but there were also a huge quantity of more ambitious things: sideboards, hutches, bars, bookcases, bunks, tables, desks, and many pieces built to special order.

BUT THE CLASSICS OF THE ENTIRE custom furniture boondoggle were surely the ornate wooden foot lockers. These were often real works of art, especially those turned out by the better carpenters in the early months of construction. These lockers were made of plywood, fashioned into enclosed boxes of a size that could be easily handled when finished. After boards were nailed or screwed together; a two to three-inch deep top piece was sawed out; hinges, catches and handles were attached and *presto!* you had a piece of functional furniture for work and home.

The wood was often burned with torches to bring out the grain, and with sanding, staining and a final coat of protection, the resulting chest was a credit to any room. Proper hardware added luster to the piece, and if a sign painter was available (not often) touches of gold paint were added to fine effect.

I really liked the chests and truly coveted one. Unfortunately, one of NANA Security's cardinal rules was that we were never to accept any gifts, and we were not to employ camp workers for any reason. It was an unwritten rule, but a strong one. At first I resented such a rule and was unhappy about having to follow it. But follow it I did. Later, I could see that it could have been no other way if I wanted to function successfully as Security.

During my last six months at Happy Valley, this unwritten rule (along with others of lesser or more importance) was relaxed and the carpenters – most of them very good friends by this time – made and installed some beautiful shelves for my rooms.

For the most part, however, my own rooms were never extravagantly decorated, especially in comparison to culinary personnel and others. My decorations ran to a gallery of photos I had taken, both in color and black and white. These were easy to transport (or store), during vacations, and added a personal touch that was daily proof I had another life aside from this one. A more colorful addition was a bouquet of huge, vivid Mexican paper flowers, (sent me by my sister, Bette) each of which could be folded into bud size for easy transport; and a few other small trifles.

Although I was never able to obtain a fancy footlocker, I did finally get a wooden electrical-wire reel. It wasn't one of the finished kind, but made an acceptable table when it was covered with an old bedspread. The reels were in high demand, excepting, of course, the huge ones. Very small and medium reels were sanded, stained and marlite tops made, and these were treasured as coffee tables, plant stands, or TV stands.

It must not be assumed that only common employees were guilty of using maintenance crews for personal projects. Some of the most ambitious remodeling went on in quarters occupied by contractors' Camp Managers. In some instances these men even had small, separate house trailers hauled in and completely furnished by the camp carpenters and electricians! Slightly below this were camp managers, all of whom rated private rooms, who simply "fixed up" the entire room. One pretentious Resident Camp Manager (RCM) had a door installed between two rooms and enjoyed a private suite.

Needless to say, the carpenters, electricians and plumbers saw to their own needs and whims and often their quarters were nearly as luxurious as those of top officials. Couples living together, or singles who did a lot of entertaining – usually young men and women in the 20 to 30 age range – generally did a lot of fixing. Often these quarters approached Arabian Harem standards, with ceilings hung with exotic Indian prints; dim, colored lights, stereos turning out soft music, fancy ceiling hangers with plants, and luxurious office chairs from warehouse supplies.

NOT BY ANY MEANS DID ALL pipeline personnel live in fancy rooms, or even attempt to fix up their quarters. It was mainly women, and men who had social lives including women, who cared about decorating the rooms. Lifelong construction workers, many of whom had lived in camps all over the world, were content to live in their small cubicles with nothing more fancy than daily maid service, which was supposed to provide cleanliness and neatness. Security's top officials, many of them sprung from military or police careers, prided themselves on living in as Spartan and functional fashion as was humanly possible. One small bag of civilian clothing for off-duty use, personal toiletries, perhaps a few books, and possibly a tape deck – that was it. They positively scorned the additional baggage toted around by their guards, especially the often excessive amounts of their female guards.

Then at the very opposite and lowest end of the scale were the men who, despite daily maid service, managed to live in filthy conditions. They were always the bane of the bullcooks' lives.

Dirty, smelly, filthy clothing, empty booze bottles, spilled food, cigarette ashes and butts, and other personal garbage was often so thick in these rooms that the poor bullcooks finally did little more than pull covers over smelly beds. Some of these men were also strangers to showering and this despite free showers and laundries offering every aid to personal cleanliness. It was the bullcooks' duty to change all sheets once a week, but before the new week was out, these beds were smelly and filthy again.

The one room that the bullcooks absolutely refused to touch belonged to a plumber and a young welder. These roommates, in an excess of ill-advised fixing, had disposed of the single bed provided and installed bunk beds with a frame of iron water pipe, which the plumber had devised. It was not only an ugly affair, but also extremely dirty to be around because the metal pipe's coating rubbed off on skin and clothing.

This unlovely piece of furniture was a source of great pride for the two men but proved so difficult and unpleasant to make up that finally the bullcooks refused to make an attempt. Since the occupants were not at all fastidious, it made no difference to them and, in the end, they continued to live in what was probably the filthiest and smelliest room in camp.

Because of the work and rules that limited my social life, I was never able to attend parties and gatherings and really observe the different remodeled rooms. However, some people left doors open for one reason or another, and I gained a glimpse occasionally. Further, when camp populations were reduced during several months of winter season I was still walking hallways and doing furnace checks. Rooms were never locked and, until carpenters had taken care of restoring them to their original shape, I could see exactly how they had been "remodeled."

Many had been completely vandalized, with closets reassembled into bars or ugly formless shapes; dressing table-desks removed or sawed apart; and un-painted shelves nailed onto fragile paneling.

The rooms, never pretty to begin with but functional and pleasant to some degree, were mauled and brutalized. Most of the occupants would never be back this way. They were like ghosts: Formless and nameless they had arrived, and so they remained. In their brief stay here, they had taken out on these inanimate objects the rages, frustrations and disappointments of life in this hard environment. To me, the scars they left behind were chilling.

These scars were almost entirely in rooms occupied by men. If the women also left scars, they seemed to be at least more constructive. Mostly they added rather than depleted. Instead of two small mirrors, women's rooms often boasted impressive arrays of mirrors, filched from other rooms, from bathrooms, and from warehouse storage. That the women did amass, and just how much, was amply proven in the fall of 1976, when Happy Valley B Camp was shut down for the winter.

Within the space of a few days a camp population of 800 to 1,100 had been reduced to zero, and only A Camp would remain open. At this point, the bullcooks lucky enough to be kept on the job were put to work divesting rooms in B Camp of all items except what they originally contained, that is, two beds and bedding, the original furniture and two mirrors. Then the excess was piled in hallways and arctic walkways.

THE AMOUNT OF STUFF PILED along the walls from the 28 rooms in the women's barracks was stunning. It ranged from clothing to all sorts of furniture both worthwhile and make shift and through every spectrum of each.

Since the bullcooks and the maintenance people were the first to reach the scene, it is logical to conclude that a lot of the choicest items had already been picked off before I arrived. One thing that interested Security was a number of containers that still held remnants of home-made wine, ample evidence that stills were not uncommon in camp. (This was no surprise, but it was still interesting.) The trash brigade was busy for days hauling the massive amount of what had been treasures to the dump and incinerator.

One particular room in the women's barracks sticks in my mind, probably because it offered a little dash of mystery. It was located at the far end of the hall and sometime after the other rooms had been cleaned and restored, I was quite certain no one had even attempted to look into it. To my knowledge no one went in or out, and the door always remained firmly locked.

At length I did some research and found that Room 28 was still registered to a Teamster who had gone on R & R, been delayed and then transferred to another camp. In view of this situation, my supervisor and the Innkeeper teamed up to investigate.

When the door was unlocked and swung open it was a latter-day scene from Doctor Zhivago that met our eyes. Thick frost coated the end and outer wall and was clinging also to objects on the walls. Some former occupant had remodeled extensively and successfully, so that the effect of the rather attractive, strange room, the thick frost and absolutely frigid air of a room that had been without heat for several months, all combined to project a somewhat romantic atmosphere. It was like a room that had been long lost and then suddenly rediscovered.

The Varied Duties of Security

It appears that a great many of the construction people here at Galbraith are pretty confused about the duties of the security guards. Some seem to think of us as some sort of bush-league policemen charged with trying to keep law and order in camp. Others see us as firemen trying to make sure the camp's buildings don't go up in flames.

Both groups are right to some extent, but there's much more to the job than just those duties. To give you an idea of what all we do, I have put together a list of some of the duties:

First of all, you have to know we were not armed. No firearms were permitted with the exception of a weapon or two in the hands of our supervisors to be used in emergency. Instead of a weapon, each guard carries a hand radio and is connected to the camp radio operator, to fellow guards and supervisors, and technically is on duty 24 hours a day.

The NANA guards are the fire watch in each camp, patrolling all barracks to check furnaces for any defects that could result in fire. A fire was much to be feared and could turn deadly, particularly when the outdoor temps were well below zero. This is the most vital of all the tasks we performed. Each of the barracks has from one to four furnaces, which are supposed to be checked at least once an hour. The outbuildings – shops, offices and so on – all have one or more furnaces that must also be checked.

Patrolling for the furnaces alone eats up a lot of my time and adds between 7 to 15 miles on every shift. But that is only part of the job.

The remaining duties add up to an amazing number and variety. My list isn't complete, but it will give you the picture. It includes jobs that face every guard at one time or another, and some, hundreds of times: report burned out lights and other electrical problems to the electricians on duty; report plumbing problems to the plumbers; prevent damage or theft of company property; keep watch for unauthorized people in camp; iron out disputes or call someone who can; discourage drinking and drug-taking prevalent at private parties after shift; direct traffic at certain times; check out-of-camp buildings such as explosives storage; check in-coming and out-going plane passengers; search for illegal alcohol when Alyeska initiates one of its periodic crackdowns on liquor in camp; herd grizzly bears, trying to keep them out of camp – or at least trying to keep bears and people apart; trying to prevent illegal parking, such as trucks on the heliport pad; loan a hand to the Medic when someone is ill or dying; keep track of all wildlife (bears, wolves, caribou) that come or attempt to come into camp; track down stolen vehicles; keep watch for oil spills in or near camp; man checkpoints in camp or on the Haul Road.

Now that is a partial list. Any situation we cannot control is placed in the hands of our sergeant or higher command. I should mention that, personally, I feel one of my extra, but important duties, is to protect women workers from any harassment.

That gives you a pretty good idea of what all we do. I find it to be an interesting job – hardly ever dull or boring – and at times even a bit exciting. When I was young, I used to spend part of my time on the ranch riding my horse and herding cattle or sheep. That can have its exciting moments, but it doesn't even come close to using a pickup truck to try and herd an 800-pound, wild and angry grizzly bear out of camp!

Here's how it goes every day (or rather night) on the job. At 6:00 p.m. we are dressed in our uniforms and report for work at the office. The night shift consists of two men and me. One man is Eric, a bright young man of 27 or so who formerly worked at McKinley Park; the other man is Gabriel, a young Eskimo from Nome, in his early 20s. From 6:00 p.m. until midnight we have a supervisor – the Sergeant – who actually works from noon until midnight. After he goes off duty, we are on our own. During the night, we each have a section of camp to check. One usually does Road Patrol in the pickup until 11:00 p.m., then checks any flights at the airport.

The guards on foot patrol walk the length of each barracks just as often as possible, while also checking out the fuel storage, shops and warehouse area. We check 200 or more furnaces for leaks and also check on the fire extinguishers, thermostats, laundry rooms (for unattended clothes irons), fire alarm systems, as well as unknown possibilities that may crop up.

Last night, in six complete rounds of the barracks, I checked out 1,200 furnaces, looking for oil leaks and so on that might cause fires. This is a continual process, going on day and night. With their constant use, and installed in temporary buildings that are by no means as firm and steady as permanent ones, furnaces can spring serious leaks in an hour or less. They can literally jolt apart.

A fire out here in the extreme cold would be very unpleasant at the least, and expensive. You can tell the cheechakoes by the way they kid us about our furnace patrol; long-time Alaskans know about fires in the North. I give these wiseacres a jolt now and then with some fire fact. We have been warned that these trailer buildings with their thin, synthetic insulation are especially hazardous; that if one catches fire, it burns with such ferocity that it will be completely consumed in *five minutes!*

When I first arrived here at Galbraith, I noticed that a large Cat tractor was parked outside the occupied barracks with the motor running day and night. The reason for this at-the-ready Cat, I was told was a precaution against fire. In that event, an operator would immediately pull the burning barracks off its foundation and away from the others.

All the fire checks keep us busy during the shift, but about once an hour or so, we check in at the office – usually having coffee and filling in part of our daily log. We can spend as much as 15 minutes an hour in the office. Then between midnight and 12:30, we eat at the messhall (lunch?), which is usually a full-size meal for the men, but not for me.

I should mention here, that on my first break last night, I was able to reach Bob on the phone. He sounded in good spirits and that made me happy because he was feeling so low when we parted at the Anchorage airport. He really didn't want me to take this job because we would be apart for so long. We never had been apart before for more than a day or two in all of our 27 years together.

We had always had the same dream and followed it together. We dreamed of moving North to the then-territory of Alaska. Once we had arrived in 1951, it became our dream to be able to explore all of the North country in Alaska and Canada and write about our experiences. Over our years in Alaska, we were able to make most of that dream come true. Going beyond the few back country roads, we studied maps and started hiking in on old trails used in pioneer days to carry the mail. This led to longer backpacking trips and eventually to a week's hiking and camping trip over the long-abandoned Chilkoot Pass Trail dating back to the 1898 gold rush.

Eventually we would make three long trips over the Chilkoot photographing the area and artifacts. We wrote several magazine articles about our trips and took pride in the fact that they helped lead the State of Alaska and Yukon Territory rehabilitation of the trail. Today the trail is part of a national park and also an international park.

All these activities were very satisfying, but as years went on we both seemed to get busier and busier and had less time for fun. Then came *Alaska Industry!*

Bob had long harbored a desire to be able to stop working for other people and editing others' publications so he could go out on his own. The very beginning of this pipeline era gave him his opportunity. He joined with three men who put out an oil industry report and formed a new corporation to publish a monthly Alaska business magazine. Bob designed the magazine, modeling it as sort of a regional version of *Business Week* but a monthly, and named it *Alaska Industry!* He wrote most of the contents of the first issue, and got it on the press. It was a success, and it was totally Bob's baby. That was the trouble: It was like a baby that seemed to need attention almost 24 hours a day, seven days a week. And it didn't seem to ever grow up or become less needful.

With Bob completely engrossed in the magazine, I felt almost abandoned. Oh, of course, I wrote an article or two for the magazine, and took some photos, but it definitely was not my baby. I had lost my traveling companion and my writing partner and I felt all alone and definitely at loose ends. So when the construction work got underway on the pipeline, and hiring boomed, I was ready for it. This could turn into *my* dream and a brand new adventure.

But what jobs were available? Which might I qualify for? It was surprisingly, frustratingly difficult to find out about work on the pipeline, either what kind was on offer, or how to get it. Office work was out for me – I loathed it and if I was going to take a job, I wanted something more active and, frankly, better paying. Surely there were other things. Bullcooking? Dishwashing? Other kitchen or housekeeping work? God knows I had the experience – a whole lifetime of it. But where to apply for such jobs? And again, if I did find one, would it pay enough and would I really want it?

I put first things first: I decided I had to make an effort to find the job first and then decide if I really wanted it. One by one I made the rounds of all possible employers. I hit Bechtel, Fluor, Alyeska, ITT, and Camp Catering. At Fluor they suggested I might qualify for a job as camp clerk at Valdez for $1,500 a month. So, back to that office work and lower pay.

Then by luck, I talked to a friend's husband who worked on the line doing construction. He mentioned something I had never thought of – Security.

"They say it pays $1,000 a week," he added.

Hmmm. Definitely interesting. So just what do they do?

"Oh, they just walk through the buildings and watch for fire hazards," he said. "*You* wouldn't want to do it! They also gather up the drunks and put them to bed. Would *you* want to rassle dirty old drunks? They do have some women but they're probably former police women."

Well, that left me out, so the search went on. The whole month of January, 1975 was a zero in my job search. So I went on to Fairbanks to try my luck there. Fairbanks was headquarters for hiring north of the Yukon River. At first, all my search there netted me was an interview with a camp catering service, again for a position as camp clerk – at $1,500 a month.

The woman who interviewed me was defensive. I made no remark about the pay, but it was obvious others had.

"I didn't realize women were so grasping," she said bitterly. "Not until I got this job."

I supposed it could have been called "ambition" in a man, but I refrained from voicing my thoughts.

After all this work, and all of the negative interviews, it was a chance meeting with a friend that actually got me a job on the line. He qualified as a "minority" and that had gotten him a pipeline job. He suggested that I put in an application with NANA Security Systems. Since it was owned by the NANA regional Native corporation, it had a certain commitment toward minorities in general, and since I was an Alaska resident and a woman – both groups officially minorities – I had that going for me.

FROM THAT MOMENT ON my long job hunt was over. Everything seemed to fall into place as neatly as if it had been foreordained, as indeed, I believed it was.

By chance, the secretary at the NANA Security office was absent when I went in to fill out the application. In her place, I was helped by Jim Messick, an interesting and friendly man, who I learned was one of the men who actually organized NANA Security. I also learned that the firm had control of all security north of the Yukon River.

After I filled out the paperwork; Messick gave me a long lecture on all the undesirable features of life on the pipeline, particularly for security people. He described the long, grueling hours; the intense cold; the isolation; the restricted life of the guards (who were expected to set an example for everyone in camp); he told me about drunks and lascivious old men who pounded on your door at night if you were a woman. The barracks rooms, he went on, were small and sparsely furnished; worst of all each room was required to have two occupants, and any roommate assigned to you might make your life completely miserable.

When he had finished the lecture I told him that none of the difficulties he outlined would stop me if I could get the job. He asked me a number of questions about my background and the types of jobs I had held. Apparently nothing I said shot me down and he could see my determination, so he told me the next step would be an interview with the boss. About ten days later I was in Fairbanks again for an interview with Bill Nix, a long-time Alaskan and a retired Alaska State Police official.

He was a quiet-spoken, grey-haired, but still youthful-looking individual. He questioned me shrewdly but not at length – Messick had apparently supplied all the details and background – then he added that they had hired several women guards with good results. And then he said:

"Yes, Mrs. Knox, and I'm going to hire you!"

That's all it took. In late March, I called his office and was told to report the following day to Fairbanks. Two days later I had gotten through all of the exams and paperwork, and I was out on the pipeline.

But what real qualifications did I have for this new job – in fact, new life – I was entering into? Besides the desire, what did I have? Jim Messick first asked that question, and in the days and weeks since that interview, the same question has been asked time and again by dozens of people. They were all curious how a petite (5 foot

1 and 112 pounds) older Alaskan housewife was able to qualify as a security guard on the Alaska pipeline. I certainly was completely lacking in any police or security experience.

The truth is, of course, that a security force is *not* a police force so that experience was not needed. Some experience or training in security or first aid would have helped. Until I got that training on the job, mostly what I had to offer was my profound willingness to learn and do the job. I had both that ambition and, I felt, a basic integrity. Maybe those showed through in my interview.

Maybe less to the point, but still worth some note, was my years of experience with wilderness isolation and construction camps. The fact I had been a writer and photographer in both outdoor and construction fields in Alaska during my long residence may have appealed in some way. At least I did know what a wilderness construction camp was and how it operated.

Also, there was little doubt that, with all my interests, I would be able to amuse and entertain myself in my off hours. On a project where two out of five people stayed only a few weeks or months and a large percentage had turned back right at the airport, my promise of longevity may have helped me. But above all, my intense desire to get the job – to get on the pipeline – must have been one determining factor.

The rest, as they say, is history. My history. It was the history also of many other women who, through necessity or choice (or both), left homes and their regular life to join the workforce on one of the world's all-time major construction projects – a job in size and scope – to be compared to digging the Panama Canal.

For many or most of them, their lives would never be the same again. And I was, to my regret, finding that it was true for me.

Sure, some women had worked on construction jobs before. But those jobs were mainly short-term as compared to the years it would take to complete the pipeline and put it into operations. And those women were very few in number when compared to thousands working on the pipeline.

Those women on former jobs were hardly countable, so few were their numbers. But now, on the pipeline, the numbers are countable: some 10% of the entire workforce are to be women. It really was far too few, and the jobs women can get are not widely enough distributed. But even so, with all of that said, it still is really a *first*. Most important of all, it marks the end forever of all-male construction jobs. And it is a step up for women in their struggle for equality.

I HAVE FELT FROM the very beginning that it could be important to make a record of my own pipeline job, from a personal standpoint as well as from that of one woman on the pipeline and what that life is like. Wherever I go, people want to know what it is all like; they want to know the common details of where we live, what the camps are like, and even what we have to eat. So my whole intent here is to tell it the way it is, without dwelling on the bizarre. Not that there aren't bizarre aspects to such a life and they do have their place in the telling.

The most bizarre aspects probably fall into three categories: those associated with the weather and the cold; the camp visits by wildlife, particularly those by grizzly bears; and the threat and dangers of fires in the camp buildings.

Let me illustrate with one minor incident that happened just a few days after I arrived in camp. It fits in the bizarre category and I will set it down just the way it appears in my journal:

> April 5: Here we sit at Galbraith on a beautiful day, and not a lick of power in camp. I awoke at 1:30 p.m. and heard an odd buzzing in the hall. Put on my robe and went out and it was the Fire Alarm System. The darned thing sure didn't sound very loud to me. It was the first time I had heard one and I wondered what to do – it was an obvious false alarm, but I had no way to shut it off. You need a key which is kept in the office.
>
> Just then Ray Leach, the day guard, arrived and took over. He said the fire alarm was set off by loss of power. The power was out all over camp. Have no idea what happened. There was still hot water, so I took a shower and washed my hair. Still no power so had to rub it dry. Once in the messhall, I asked one of the cooks what happened about food and he said prep all

came to a stop. Dinner will either be late or have to be cold cuts. He said once last winter a power outage lasted so long that they were thinking of evacuating the whole camp. At 60 or 70 below, this camp would freeze up tighter than a drum. You can imagine how fast these metal units would cool off at 60 below!

That's the journal entry. But not the end of the story. At 3:55 the power came back on and everything returned to normal. Regular lights were on and so forth. Fortunately they do have an emergency light system. Part of my duties is to check all of these lights. Believe me, I am more and more impressed with the importance of Security – I believe we are about the most important people in camp!

To complete the story: At 4:30 p.m. the power went off once again and the fire alarm again started up, driving me bonkers. I had to run over to the office to get a key to shut it off.

It seemed to me that, all in all, that day qualified on the bizarre side.

NANA's Dress Code

What unhappiness I suffered during my first days on the job at Galbraith was due to the uniform I had to wear while on shift. It wasn't the fault of the uniform itself but the fact that it was just such a poor fit and made me look and feel like some kind of a scarecrow.

Much of the mental and physical conversion from civilian life into the world of the security guard is via the uniform. Not only is the guard affected by the uniform he wears, but all who come into contact with the uniformed guard are also affected. My conversion came with its own bumps and strains because, on that first day in Fairbanks when we were outfitted and only men's uniforms were available.

To say that my looks were changed by the uniform is a gross understatement. The men's uniforms left a good deal to be desired for most women. In my own case, at five feet one inch and 112 pounds, the smallest size draped, dragged, and drooped. Jackets and trousers both required major tailoring jobs, but there was no time for me to do it or get it done. As a consequence, for the first nine weeks, I went on duty looking atrocious and suffering mental tortures because of it. (After the first nine weeks we changed to lighter summer uniforms, and by the following fall I had altered the winter uniforms to fit.)

The NANA winter uniforms were grey woolen twill in the classic style of the "Alaskan Tuxedo" long treasured by construction workers and bush travelers in the far North. Tuxedo jackets were characterized by straight, trim lines, with four front pockets with snaps; and the entire double back is a huge pocket, with zippers under the arms for access. The trousers are trim and straight with generous pockets.

To complete this outfit, we wore grey work shirts. From the beginning I obtained permission to wear white turtle-neck sweaters (a few male guards adopted this; others wore white T-shirts). With this touch of white and the white hard hats we wore during construction, I was well satisfied with how I looked. The summer uniforms were wash and wear grey trousers, the same work shirts, and short dark blue jackets.

All security uniforms had to have identification patches. The NANA patch was as Alaskan as the Eskimos from whom it originated: A black and white drawing of an Eskimo seal hunter in parka and mukluks, his spear in his left hand. This really neat-looking patch was on the upper left sleeve of the jacket and parka; in smaller size above the left breast shirt pocket and on the flat front surface of hard hats. Other than the elegant patch, NANA uniforms were free of gee-gaws; no stripes, badges, whistles, chains, braid or ties. I felt they were refreshingly Alaskan, harmonious with the country and the project. Quite frankly, I was proud of mine and always felt good about wearing it.

In addition to the esthetic value, the woolen, tightly woven material was warm and of fine quality that held creases reasonably well. The grey did not show dirt easily, so that two pairs of trousers and one jacket actually held up well for nine weeks between R & Rs and a visit to the dry cleaners.

Everyone who traveled to the line was required to have a down-filled Arctic parka. Ours were especially nice, of deep green shiny material with good wolf ruffs (wolf fur resists frost); and were fastened with full-length zippers and buttons. Again, they were sized for men. As a result, mine was capacious, reaching below my knees, when it should have been above the knees or even mid-thigh.

Bundled in my parka and hard hat, I was aware I caused some smiles, no doubt resembling a perambulating green tent with a cone of snow on top.

"Where did you get that parka?" someone would ask. "Just a little bit long isn't it?"

Came the cold weather and the remarks were somewhat the same but the meaning was different:

"Where did you get that long parka? That's nice, keeps your legs warm!"

In between parka weather and spring clothing, we wore down vests, which gave considerable warmth coupled with freedom of movement. Any odd-colored personal parkas were taboo.

Footgear and gloves were up to our own discretion. I preferred washable knit gloves, for mostly we were not outside of warm buildings or vehicles long enough to make mittens necessary. Shoe pacs were the favorite footgear. These boots have rubber feet and leather uppers, and heavy felt liners and innersoles that can be removed each night for drying out. When worn with insulated socks they are extremely warm, though bulky. Perhaps their biggest drawback was lack of firm grip, so that on ice they were hazardous. After two nasty spills, I wore them only during extreme cold when ice and snow were less slippery. For the most part, my footwear was lightweight waffle stompers with Vibram soles that clung to most all surfaces. With heavy socks, these proved plenty warm.

Inner clothes were entirely up to the individual, as were off-duty garments. During -30 to -50 or more, even the warm twill trousers needed long underwear underneath to be comfortable. Summer and winter I wore panty hose, which added warmth and, almost as important, protection from the rough trouser material.

One last item of clothing that was issued in camp, was the hardhat liner. Made of warm, flannel-like material shaped to fit the inside of the hard hat, with snaps to secure them, and ear flaps that could be folded down and fastened under the chin for warmth, or up for hearing, liners were the only thing that made our metal head gear bearable in extreme cold. At 40 to 60 below zero, hardhats seemed to absorb and generate cold.

Dressed for winter in underclothes, pantyhose, long johns, heavy socks and shoe pacs, white blouse and work shirt, trousers, jacket, parka, hard hat and gloves, and carrying a flashlight, hand radio, pencil and pad and a Tower of London-type bunch of keys, it is little wonder that each guard weighed in at a number of pounds over actual body weight. But running up and down stairs, walking up to 15 miles a shift, and climbing into and out of pickups did help to burn up all of those extra calories.

Chapter 6

Characters in Camp

Jean, my roommate, has left on R & R. It is her first, and she was so excited, I never thought she'd make it to the plane, that she'd just probably collapse. Jean's husband is with the Fairbanks city police. The reason she is working here, is to help pay off a huge, expensive house they're building out in a Fairbanks suburb.

Never thought I'd say this, but I'm sure going to miss her. I'll miss the little chats we were able to have just in passing. It does get lonesome at times here all by myself. Of course, there are quite a few interesting characters here in camp that I can afford to spend a little time with, without getting too friendly. Sort of impersonal, personal.

Galbraith is sort of in a unique position – just about midpoint between Fairbanks and the end of the line at Prudhoe – so that it attracts a lot of top company officials and visiting firemen. That has good points, as well as bad. It means everyone pretty much has to keep on their toes with no slacking off, but that also includes the cooks, which means we are treated to really excellent meals. The camp's midpoint location also means that it seems to have more than its share of interesting characters, both visiting and local.

For instance, down in the generator shop, a couple of men are on duty 24 hours a day (that's two for each shift). They are usually bored out of their minds – with nothing to do except punch a button on the hour.

One of the generator men, who I see on the night shift, is an interesting character, who actually owns a lodge on the Denali Highway. During the long, boring hours he has used odd bits of wood and carved a five-dog team, sled and musher.

The carving is simply beautiful, and fairly large. The sled is probably nine to 12 inches long and complete down to the last detail. The dogs are in proportion and just darling, each different in some way. The musher, who has his feet on the runners and his mittened hands on the back of the sled is excellent in detail although faceless. The dog harness is rawhide and the lines are made out of braided string; red, so they supply some color. All the details are perfect to the last notch. It could be a sensation in a tourist shop and would be quite priceless.

The people here are not by any means all construction types. Many have widely varied talents in different fields, and are interesting in their own ways. One young kid (there are many young kids here) explained his job to me this way:

"All I do is stir shit all day."

He works at the sewage treatment plant. In civilian life he has a degree in drama from the University of Washington, but has been working his gold claim some 60 miles north of Fairbanks. He wants me, while on R & R, to find him a horse to buy so he can pack supplies in to his claim.

There's a nice old gal from North Pole, who I chat with on my rounds. There's a pretty young gal at the mess hall who previously did office work. Also, two young female archeologists.

In our own NANA outfit, we have a handsome young man who is a lawyer when not working on the pipeline. Another of our guards is an older man of 60 or so, who is an old-time showman. He is a musician who served in the navy as a bandmaster and boasts of his band playing aboard the *USS Missouri* during the Japanese surrender ceremony that ended World War II. Then in civilian life he went on to play the sax with some big bands.

So I would say we have a real conglomeration here at Galbraith – people colorful and fascinating! I meet them all on my rounds and will know each and every person in camp before it's over.

Just the other day a young man spoke to me. He said he had noticed my hard hat, which is white with a black-and-white NANA insignia and my full name. He introduced himself as Jim Knox. He said I was the only other Knox he had ever met. He's from Eagle River and his folks are from Scotland. He's a pre-med student and is working here to help pay his college expenses. He has a job as a ground controller at the airport.

I just want to add something about the musician I mentioned earlier. His name is Ray Leach and he is well-liked here at the NANA office, and the other day we learned it was his birthday. We scurried around and tried to figure out how we could have some kind of a party for him. Ray is a diabetic, which made things kind of difficult, but Jean located a case of 24 cans of Fresca – which he can drink – and we gave him that, a card we had all signed, and a doughnut with one candle. Not very fancy, but Ray enjoyed it.

PROBABLY THE BIGGEST character of all the people in camp is a little old guy who nobody even notices. He is a scrawny little guy who is the bullcook who does the building where our office is located. He goes by the name of Bud, and that's all the name we know.

Bud is really a professional bullcook and camp worker. He has been working for years and years all over the Alaska outback. He is the type who just fades into the background of camp life and nobody (except perhaps Eric and myself) ever really notices him. He is always on the job, plugging along and saying very little – unless you stop and talk. Then he will start telling you stories as he leans on his mop or wipes out ashtrays. He punctuates his narratives with frequent spurts of tobacco juice into the trash can or even right into his mop water.

Bud first came to Alaska from Wisconsin and he still has scads of relatives back there. Over his years of bullcooking in Alaska he has saved his money and spent it on choice farm land back in Wisconsin. He gets a faraway look in his eyes as he tells you that one of these days he's going to pack it in and retire to his farm and raise Herefords. With a touch of pride, he tells you that his farm is worth some $300,000, but Bud still plugs along mopping, dreaming of the fancy, great silo he plans to buy for his farm, and of that day when he can quit all this and spend the rest of his life farming. God knows how old he is now – maybe 45, maybe 50.

Bud has worked at Point Barrow and Barter Island and many remote camps in the Arctic. Often he spent long stretches working without taking any leave in order to save up money for the farm. For instance he spent 26 months straight at Barter Island without R & R and thought nothing of it.

He certainly qualifies as an old-timer, or as we like to say, a "Real Sourdough!" I particularly like talking to people like him and now, with almost 25 years of traveling around Alaska, I can pass myself off as just another *real* Alaskan. Anyhow I'm all for people like Bud, and I hope that soon he will be able to start living his dream and spend the rest of his days on his farm.

There are very few people as interesting as Bud, but I try to talk to everyone on my rounds. I threw myself into this – seeing it as a real part of my job and I think I've done a pretty good public relations job for NANA. I have learned that the company had a pretty poor image here when the security guards were all men. My roommate Jean is a very outgoing person and helped change that image dramatically. And in the few weeks I have been here, I believe I have added a lot to that. That's not boasting. The fellows (my co-workers) told me that and it makes me feel *good*. This is certainly a very curious job.

While I do try to talk to everyone on my rounds – and almost everyone is friendly and happy to chat – I do have to mention the one or two exceptions I have run into. These were old-time construction workers and they both had the same beef: Women on the job. The first man with whom I had been exchanging late night-shift conversation looked pleasant enough, a blondish, wiry man who must have been around 50. It is only when I mention women workers that he explodes into bitterness:

"I don't mind telling you," he almost shouted, "that I just don't approve of women on the line! It's no place for 'em! They shoulda stayed at home. They can't do the job!"

"How long have you been in construction?" I asked, hiding the anger seething inside.

"It's been 25 years now, but not much longer," he said sort of proudly. I've bought a condo and I'm gonna retire there any day now."

You bastard, I thought to myself. I'd sure like to have a condominium in Hawaii; and if I'd been able to work in construction for 25 years I could sure have one.

Scene Two, same place, different man but same type. He was older, more handsome, soft spoken. We were discussing the Laborers' Union, to which I belonged during construction, and to which he also belonged.

"I'm going to work long enough to be vested for retirement," I told him.

"I don't believe in women in the Laborers' Union,"he said mildly but firmly. "They never should have let women in. They can't do Laborers' jobs."

I am surprised and shocked, but he continues without waiting to hear my reaction:

"They grab all the soft jobs. I think of all the poor old work-worn laborers who *need* such jobs as flagmen, when they get so poorly they can't do much else. They deserve those soft jobs."

Again I'm seething. I can think of at least two women in my close circle of friends, who spent their entire lives raising large families, without even Social Security to look forward to, and were then left destitute through divorce. What happens to all the poorly old women who need soft jobs?

I walk away still seething inside, but happy too, that this man – like the first one – is part of a small minority and already an anachronism – at least in his way of thinking. Hopefully those days will never return and women will achieve a bit of equality.

Well, maybe it is time for these two men, and others of the same type, to drag up and retire to those condos in Hawaii. They are surely living in the past.

Like I said earlier, this surely is a very curious job and you certainly get to meet all types of people.

Empty Rooms & Fire Alarms

It is true that the work of a security guard on the Arctic section of the pipeline is indeed a curious job. Many things help to make it unusual and curious work, but two that contribute in large part are empty barracks and false fire alarms.

To illustrate that, let me describe one unusual night shift just the way I set down in my journal:

It's 2:00 a.m. and only four more hours to go. My Vibram-soled boots make soft, squinchy echoes down the arctic walkway as I approach Barracks W. At the heavy fire door I pause, pulling the wolf ruff of my down parka close against my face where it feels as warm as if the wolf himself was still inside, then stand on tiptoe to look in the small window of the door. Directly on the other side is a small vestibule of rough boards, perhaps 12X6 feet in size. To the left, a crash-barred door leads outside; but it is the long, white hallway stretching beyond the inner glass door that claims my attention. Thirty-eight doors march down the white-walled hallway which is brightly lighted by small decorative lights above the doors.

Opening the fire door I step into the

vestibule where thick cold hits my face and lungs with the shock-freshness of cold water. Inside the door I reach into the depths of my parka pocket and bring out my walky-talky, carefully adjusting volume and squelch buttons until I am surrounded by a cocoon of noise. Inside this reassuring safety pocket I start cautiously down the long, empty hallway of the deserted barracks.

My footsteps sound loud in the peculiar, eerie emptiness. Outside it is -20 degrees on this Arctic April night. That cold makes the metal and wood modular units creak and groan and it sounds like brittle pistol shots, audible above my radio's pocket of sound.

At each of the doors, fear clutches at my throat. My fingers tighten about the flashlight in my right hand and the radio in my left.

The closed doors are no worry—just the open ones. Suppose someone has opened the door in preparation for my passing, and poises ready to jump out? I whip by the yawning room, its beds and stingy dressers lurking in shadow.

But who would be lurking in these cold, unfinished trailers at two in the morning? Drunks? Rapists? Murderers?

Sensible arguments are of no avail.

I pray for the day when the hallway will be warm and carpeted. And then on the other side of each door two peaceful persons will be sleeping sweetly.

I am almost at the end now. Should I go the rest of the way or cut my patrol short? Who would ever know if I just cut it short?

"You would, you coward!"

Only two more doors. To bolster my courage, I turn up the squelch until it booms against the walls. Gratefully I reach the end of the hall and turn back. The return trip is less harrowing. I breathe a sigh of relief as I turn the door knob and open the door to go outside. But just then the radio came to life:

"Security 3! Security 3! Fire alarm in A Barracks!"

It was mandatory for me now to drop every other task and head fast as possible by the closest route to A Barracks. Every other guard in camp and on duty was to do likewise.

No matter what the time, early a.m. or early p.m. all efforts had to be directed toward finding the source of the alarm. Halls, laundry rooms, bathrooms and the furnace rooms were hastily checked for smoke or for an activated smoke sensor, which usually had a small red light that started blinking. If the guilty sensor was not found, every room in the building had to be inspected visually.

Since the Fireman on duty at the time also responded to the radio alert, that often created a three-ring circus effect in the barracks with guard(s) and fireman knocking on doors (in the case of 56- man barracks this meant 28 rooms to inspect) often while being cursed out by the rudely-awakened occupants.

As it turned out, that alarm I raced to in A barracks was just another false alarm. Far, far more false alarms occurred than real alarms. There were many varied reasons for all the false alarms. During my early days at Galbraith, it was discovered that the entire employee roster of one electrical contractor was engaged in setting off false alarms. They were doing it not only to harass the security guards, but mainly so they would be called out at overtime pay rates, since it was the maintenance electricians who had to be called to re-set the alarms. Such malicious mischief was recognized almost at once, but it seemed little could be done about it. However, it was a fact that this same contractor was soon shipped off the line, after which false alarms declined greatly.

Many of the other false alarms I responded to were set off by excessive pipe, cigarette, or joint smoke in a room where several people had gathered for an after-hours party. Given enough smoke in one small room (especially in winter when windows were tight shut), and a sensor would go off.

Then there were the odd-ball ones. Like the time some men were bringing out the grain in a new table with an acetylene torch. Another time a careless sleeper placed a candle in a paper cup and it burned through the cup and into the table beneath while the misguided occupant slept peacefully nearby and could have resulted in a real tragedy. Another time, flammable fabric draped over a bare light bulb to create special color effects caused smoke and alarms.

Causes of false alarms, not the least of which were simple malfunction, were as many and varied as the occupants of rooms in the barracks. But they *all* had to be checked out carefully because among those hundreds of false alarms there might someday be real cause for alarm. An alarm that could be a life-threatening disaster.

IT CAME ON A TYPICAL winter night while I was working at Happy Valley A Camp, just 90 miles south of Prudhoe. Outside, it was a nippy -30 degrees and thankfully calm, as I made my rounds in the warm complex where the messhall and rec room were located. Suddenly I heard the voice of Betty, the radio operator, on my handy-talky:

"Security 3! Security 3! Check the Arctic Contractor's office – we have a fire alarm!"

"Security 3 on the way," I acknowledged, running across the rec room, throwing open the doors to the vestibule and then outside.

A massive dose of adrenaline shot into my system: Orange flames as tall as the sky danced across the roof of the arctic walkway linking the living quarters – three 52-

man barracks – and the office-radio room complex, directly cross the yard from me.

It was 14 minutes before midnight and in those three barracks roughly 150 people lay sound asleep. The few night persons around were in the messhall behind me having lunch. It was not a party night. I had already checked the barracks furnaces a number of times. I knew how quiet it was and not a soul inside to alert the sleepers. After all those thousands of false alarms – now this!

"My God," I screamed into my radio, "this is a *real fire*. The offices and walkway are on fire!"

At that time we had a shortage of guards. I was not certain where my sergeant was, but it didn't matter. The only other guard on duty was over in B camp, nearly a half mile away across the Haul Road.

I knew it rested squarely on my shoulders to get the occupants of those three barracks awake and outside. Bursting into the arctic walkway I found thick smoke but no flames as yet. Still on the run, I crashed into N Barracks pounding doors furiously.

"Get out! Wake up! Get outside! It's a real fire!"

It was my barracks too and my roommate, a woman, was there asleep. To this day I find it incredible that she and others responded so poorly to what came so close to a catastrophic event. With the exception of one man, who swiftly appeared in a minimum of clothes and automatically started helping me alert the sleepers, not a soul offered to help.

With N Barracks finally getting moving, I ran back into the walkway only to find smoke now so thick I couldn't even make it the few feet to M Barracks. Only one solution came to mind. I raced back down M, then outside and to the back door of M. Then I repeated it with L Barracks.

It was a pleasant surprise that our fire department responded so fast and so efficiently. Between the firemen and a few volunteers, the blaze was under control in about 45 minutes. The loss was mainly to the offices across from the barracks.

The reactions of the barracks residents were far less exemplary than those of the fire department. All of the occupants did go outside. Many opened the windows and tossed out their belongings and several simply jumped out the windows behind their possessions. Most, once they found the fire was in the offices, persisted in returning by way of the back door to retrieve belongings despite my pleas to keep the back doors shut to prevent very dangerous draft conditions.

To me the most astonishing feature of the episode was another reaction by the residents of the barracks – not all of course – but the majority. One by one they came to me that night and offered me personal thanks for "saving" them. I was touched and hardly knew what to say because I never had any thought of being heroic; and the barracks did not burn, although they did come within a hair's breadth of it. Even the Resident Camp Manager, the most important person in camp, and a rather fearsome individual, complimented me repeatedly for what I had done and forever after until the end of his tenure at the camp, always addressed me as Kiddo!.

My sergeant, in his weekly report, wrote at the end of a description of the fire: "Guard Knox's conscientiousness and observations were especially commendable."

It is an interesting epilogue to this incident that the fire actually was caused by a furnace that exploded. I had checked the furnace earlier, found it operating in a faulty manner and called the night plumber. Although this man worked on the furnace, he failed to stand by, as was required, for a sufficient amount of time to make sure it was operating properly. It was rumored that this plumber was heavily into drugs.

In the end, the man lost his job. When the final reports for the cause of the $120,000 fire were made out, it was I who made the detailed report for security.

As I pointed out earlier, a typical shift for a security guard was apt to be filled with 12 hours of walking, checking furnaces, and monotonous repetition. That kind of monotony prevented many fires and other disasters, but it was not for everyone. Not all guards responded well to this routine work. It required self-discipline and a deep sense of responsibility, which were not strong points with a lot of people, regardless of age, sex, or background. Although I regarded my job as a real challenge, I was well aware that, to many, the real challenge was successful goofing off.

I cannot resist describing one incident, which in a sense was the classic comic prototype of a Security goof-off. It happened one warm spring day when an over-zealous forklift driver inadvertently hooked his rig onto a door and pulled the whole front end off a small warehouse. The swift and surprising result was like some artist's slice-through picture to permit the viewer to see the whole inside of a building. And what did this warehouse slice-through reveal? A NANA Security Guard (a young male) sitting in cozy solitude in a chair on the second floor, reading a book!

Barracks and warehouses were by no means the only areas around the camps that had to be throughly checked for fire and other potential hazards. Wherever there was activity or materials stored, inspections took place. Storage areas, inside and outside; mechanics' shops, and especially the POL areas where huge amounts of gasoline and oil were stored, both in tanks and bladders, had to be eyeballed regularly. We watched for leakage or unusual activity everywhere. Many areas were so potentially explosive that one small leak and a carelessly tossed match, or the spark from an exhaust, could have resulted in loss of life or a huge loss of property.

It was one of our guards whose sharp lookout spotted the oil leak near Galbraith that ran into the thousands of gallons. (Since Alyeska tried to hush up or minimize news about oil spills, the extent of this one was never actually released to anyone.)

Waking across the tundra between buildings one day in early summer, he spotted oil seeps coming out of the ground some distance from buildings or visible pipe. But this was only the tip of the iceberg.

Ultimately an ugly 10-foot-deep trench had to be excavated and one whole section of camp had to be evacuated. Burn-off in the trench was still going on months later, while despite all efforts to prevent it, oil ran down the beautiful stream flowing into Galbraith Lake itself.

Chapter 7

The cause of this catastrophe was sheer careless-
ness and the inability of employees and department heads
to calculate how much oil was actually needed to heat a
block of buildings. For many months fuel trucks depos-
ited oil in tanks for one complex, only to have it disappear amazingly fast. What had happened below the
buildings was that a buried line had ruptured and the majority of oil simply ran into the ground. Eventually such
a huge amount of oil had to reappear somewhere, and
those were the seeps our guard had discovered.

Not all of Security's checks were made directly in
camp. Sometimes we had powder magazines that had to
be kept locked, and these were always miles out of camp.
Other camps also had a burn area where certain kinds of
trash were disposed of by fire, and these were inspected
several times each shift. Material stored out in the field
in isolated areas; the Haul Road, where accidents often
occurred; the pipeline itself; all came under Security's
scrutiny.

Not a little of Security's time and efforts involved
work at the camp airport. All arrivals and departures had
to be carefully attended. We stood by while the plane
landed, ready to give a hand in case of emergency, along
with the camp's fire department. Then a guard stood at
the foot of the ramp as passengers came down, sometimes – in fact, quite often – checking ID badges, since
one unflagging rule throughout construction was that
each person coming into camp had to be authorized to do
so.

Other reasons for attending loading and unloading
included making sure no one was smoking; and since

nearly all flights just made momentary stops and engines were not shut down, passengers were watched to make sure they didn't get near a propeller or an area where heavy freight was being handled.

During the frequent and long intervals when Alyeska attempted to wipe out drinking in the camps, we were to question and even inspect "suspicious-looking" pieces of luggage or baggage that might contain booze. Also, during an extended period of time when Alyeska was trying to get at the root of a serious tool thievery problem, our guards had to inspect nearly every piece of luggage that left camp before stamping the pieces okay for loading. This turned into a very big project, especially when the camp was as huge as Galbraith or Happy Valley.

Needless to say, these inspections for booze or tools were highly unpopular with the arriving or departing passengers. They often created highly explosive situations. Instead of realizing that the guards had no choice but to carry out their assigned duties, the camp residents often held them personally responsible for the annoyances and inconvenience of these unpopular inspections. Alyeska officials themselves – usually ones in some minor capacity – often were just as incensed as the camp residents.

The truth is, of course, that booze always appeared in large amounts, and tools in large amounts disappeared in ways Security couldn't control – over the Haul Road. Even if Security had a staff big enough to stop and search every truck, the powerful Teamsters Union would never have permitted it.

Chapter 7

So as time went on and Alyeska came up with its periodic crackdowns, the security guards continued to be cursed at and maligned, as they bore the brunt of a distasteful and really futile searching charade. All of the searching turned up a very negligible amount of stolen tools or other Alyeska property. Meanwhile "hot goods" continued to make the trip south via the Haul Road.

As to the booze, let's just say there never seemed to be any shortage for all the after-shift parties in all the camps.

The Undershorts Desperado

The Security Guard system during the construction of the pipeline was not set up as a police agency. Rather, the intention was to provide personnel who would have the job of guarding the pipeline system, the camps, and the workers from possible fires or other disasters and even from encounters with wandering wildlife. But even so, there were times when the Guards had to engage in what might be called police activities, such as the Case of Undershorts Man!

It happened one mid-evening in July when Galbraith Camp hung suspended in the shimmering foothills of the Brooks Range. Heat, from 14 hours of summer sunshine, made the barracks uncomfortable. It was not a party night, but small groups of day workers murmured behind half-closed doors. Muted music and sweet pot smoke curled into hallways.

I have been checking barracks and furnaces for an hour and a half when I step into an arctic hallway and see a man, naked except for his undershorts, disappearing into the foyer of the women's barracks. What goes – why is this guy parading around in public places clad only in his shorts?

I have seen plenty of men in shorts going between their rooms and bathrooms; but going from barracks to barracks is strictly against the rules. As he turns into P Barracks he glances back, he has a face with pitted skin, and wiry black hair. He seems slightly shifty.

I am apprehensive. Should I call for help over my radio? As far as I know he has done nothing wrong, but his intentions seem dubious. He walks on, walking slowly through the barracks, glancing back now and then. I keep my distance but leave him no doubt he is being followed. Passing the women's restroom I note the doors are closed, but one opens cautiously and Fran the bull-cook peers out of the slit, her eyes wide.

"What happened?" I asked.

"I was just leaving the restroom," Fran said, "when I saw him knock on my door. So I ducked back in here. This is the second time he's been here," she whispers.

"Well, you can go to your room now. I'll follow him and make sure he doesn't come back again," I assured her.

"I don't even know him! I'm sure glad you came along," she said, and ran for her room.

I continued on and got outside in time to see the Undershorts Desperado whisk into R Barracks, throwing me one last dirty look. He is nowhere to be seen when I walk in, but a door is closing down the hallway and I hurry along to get the number on the door. Back at my office it is an easy matter to look at a list of camp residents and find who occupies this room. There will be an IR (Incident Report) filed.

As it happened, the Undershorts Desperado was never heard from again. Such police activities took up a very small part of our work. To give you the whole picture I must explain that I can only speak for the Arctic section of the pipeline project during construction days. The way it was organized was that security on the whole line from Prudhoe to Valdez was split into two sections with the dividing line at the Yukon River. South of the Yukon, the security work was handled by Wackenhut, an international security company based in Miami, Florida.

North of the Yukon, security was under the juris-diction of NANA (Native Association of Northern Alaska) a corporation formed by the native villagers of the far North and Arctic. NANA's section was in two parts, with the southern section covering from Five Mile Camp, near the Yukon on north to, but not including Chandalar, on the northern flank of the Brooks Range. The section included everything from Chandalar to Prud-hoe.

I can't speak about the Wackenhut operation south of the Yukon, and even the southern district of NANA is outside my experience for the most part and can only re-ceive passing notice. Excepting for one tour at Five Mile, I saw little of the southern operations. Quite frankly, one tour in that area was enough for me for a number of reasons, chief of these being that I had formed a real love affair with the Arctic country north of the Brooks. In addition, I knew the people in the north, and the supervisors there, and I simply felt happier and more at home.

None of these reasons were really legitimate, of course, so I am still very much aware that it was a stroke of luck – and one I am still grateful for – that my request to return north was granted.

While I know that most of NANA's security work and procedures were similar in the two sections, there were differences – some very subtle – and I therefor confine my descriptions and comments (except where noted) to the northern Arctic section. In fact, since this is documentary in nature, I feel justified in limiting the over-all picture to the camps I knew best: Galbraith, Happy Valley and Toolik.

In this section, then, we had an Area Supervisor, Capt. Bernard "Barney" Carr, who reported to the NANA Security Systems Manager at the head office in Fairbanks. Captain Carr, a retired Army colonel, was in his late 40s or early 50s. It was his duty to rove his section, staying at the various camps but maintaining his own head office at Happy Valley.

Below Captain Carr was at least one lieutenant, at the time I arrived, Jim Miller; and at each of the camps a day sergeant and a night sergeant. Then there were guards of a number suitable to the season and occasion, for each of the two 12-hour shifts.

It is really not inappropriate to liken our security set-up to a hive of bees, with the captain as the queen, the lieutenant and sergeants the drones, and the guards as the workers.

It is more difficult to describe just what we did and didn't do during our 12-hour shifts. Such episodes as the one with the undershorts desperado were the rare and unusual tasks. Most of the tasks were pretty cut and dried. At the top of the list was the fire watch in barracks, office complexes and every other area in the camp, inside and out. It struck me then and still persists in my mind that the fire-watch was the most demanding and worthwhile part of the job.

But despite our busyness with fire safety, that was still only one of the myriad tasks assigned to us. One of the other really difficult and demanding jobs was our role as public relations experts with the entire camp population. We had to know and preferably be on good (but not intimate) terms with everybody in camp. In effect, we were the mothers and fathers of the camps, trying to keep track of what the kids were doing, the better to catch them if they were doing wrong in any way that might endanger other residents or camp property.

This often required us to do a juggling act of the finest sort and enough tight-rope walking to challenge a circus performer.

We were the information service for residents and visitors; the liaison department between residents (and sometimes visitors) and every single department head and maintenance person in camp. We unlocked doors for those who locked themselves out; adjusted heat or had it adjusted; operated a lost and found department; aided the Inn-Keeper in keeping rooms assigned right.

It was also part of our job to see that every single appliance, light bulb, toilet and so on was in top – or near top – working order.

If someone was seriously ill in our camp, we helped the medic in every way possible, according to our varied first aid experience (and some of our people had extensive experience). If the sick or injured person should die, we notified the proper authorities; locked up his or her personal belongings, inventoried them, packed them, and sent them to the coroner in Fairbanks.

If someone was drunk in public, high on dope, out of his mind, harassed the women, grew grass in his room, gambled indiscreetly, yanked a toilet out of the wall in a fit of pique, wrecked one of Alyeska's vehicles, started a fire, kept his barracks awake half the night, went joy-riding, didn't show up for work, carved someone up with a knife (all of these things did happen) they required action by Security. If the guard couldn't handle the situation, the sergeant took over; if the sergeant was stymied; the lieutenant or captain was called, either in person in camp, or in a pinch, over the telephone for advice and instructions.

In addition to these and dozens of other impromptu situations that could and did crop up regularly among the human residents of camp, we were also charged with protecting the wild visitors to the camps. These included the foxes, wolves, caribou, wolverines, parky squirrels, and most important of all, the grizzly bears.

There were strict camp rules against humans harassing, killing, molesting or befriending any wild animal and while there were no laws governing the actions of the animals against humans, this was of vital interest to us also. Security was the buffer between the two factions and thus it was that all the guards had to spend a surprising amount of time throughout the spring, summer and fall as animal and particularly grizzly bear herders.

DESPITE THE GENEROUS HELPINGS of exotic fare such as herding grizzlies, and the always and forever war we waged on minor and major camp crime, for the most part our 12-hour per day, 7-day per week, and 9-week tours brought more monotony and drudgery than the average non-pipeliner could ever imagine in his wildest dreams. And sheer, devastating, bone-deep weariness of both mind and body.

Throughout most of my 26-month job with security during construction days I worked as a night guard. My shift started at 6:00 or 6:30 p.m., lasting until the same time the following morning. I might add here that guards were actually on call for 24 hours a day. If needed in an emergency we might work a shift and a half or even two or more without sleep.

My "day" actually started when my alarm went off and woke me about 2:00 or 2:30 p.m. Sleeping in camp, especially day sleeping, was seldom totally restful, due to the noise and continual activity of both humans and machinery. A compassionate waitress, who also worked nights, taught me to use wax earplugs, and then gave me a handful she had left over. To Chocey I owe a debt of gratitude, for without her help I might never have survived those 26 months.

Even at the best though, my four to six-hour "sleeps" were all too short and each awakening was really painful.

It took a whole lot of will power just to drag myself out of bed and it took strong measures to pull myself together for the upcoming shift. The only way I could throw aside the weariness of the previous shift was to head immediately for the bathroom and take a long, hot shower (seldom less than 15 minutes) followed by a dash of cold. At that time I was wearing a blow-dry hair-do so quite often I also shampooed.

Then I hastily dressed in fresh civilian clothing and headed for the messhall or mug-up room for coffee and fresh fruit. This was my breakfast, eaten often in the company of other night people and/or simply goof-offs on coffee breaks.

One of the things I sorely missed on night shift was a real breakfast and I often dreamed of bacon, eggs, toast and the like. But in all the nights I worked only one camp offered breakfast to night people, and this only at the peak of the work season.

It was seldom that all this rising, showering, dressing and messhall interlude occupied less than one and a half hours, and that brought my time up to nearly four in the afternoon.

That left one hour – or at the very most two – for doing laundry, writing letters, going for a walk, taking pictures, reading, or simply loafing, before dinner-time and the shift change.

IF WE WERE LUCKY AND HAD a humane culinary manager and crew, night workers were sometimes served in advance of the messhall's official opening, which varied between 5:30 and 6:00 p.m. If we were unlucky, we might find we had to wait until 10 or 15 minutes before we had to be at work, resulting in only a few minutes to be served our food and then eat the main meal of the day.

In any event, some security supervisors allowed us to wear our uniforms to dinner (though uniforms at other times when off duty were forbidden), and I then wore mine, as did many of the other guards, most of whom slept until half an hour or less before shift. It was then necessary only to swing by my room for hat and parka before reporting to the security office shortly before shift change.

Here the off-going and on-coming shifts went through a ritual dictated by the current supervisor, which usually meant a briefing of vital news by the off-going guards, who passed along radios supplied with freshly-charged batteries.

I then took a few minutes to fill out the start of a daily log, noting name, date, time and area of patrol. Setting out, I checked in by radio with a fellow guard, or the operator in the radio room, to make certain my radio was in good operating order for, of all the equipment and paraphernalia the guards carried or wore, none was more important and vital than his walky-talky.

It is astonishing to most people that during the pipeline construction days the guards were unarmed. (This was not true later on. Once the pipeline went into operation we guards received firearms training and carried sidearms.) During construction, all firearms were banned in camp, except for a few rifles and/or shotguns kept under lock and key and the supervision of security officials. In those days the radios were vitally important for the safety of the guards, who daily faced a wide range of humanity and situations, as well as wild animals. They were equally as important – or even more so – for the safety of the whole camp and every person in it.

Another 12 hours of work looming before me, I then set out on the night's first round of checking barracks, offices and related buildings. My vital companion

– my radio – tucked securely in a holster carried on a strap from right shoulder to left waist.

I made a fast, thorough inspection of every furnace in my entire area. Not only was it a visual inspection, but a smell, touch, audial inspection as well. Each guard was to assume that the off-going guard had been unable or just unwilling to make such a close inspection (since furnace inspection was not universally popular with the guards this was not infrequently true, added to which was the fact that that the tag-end of a 12-hour shift did not promote conscientiousness in all guards). My inspection, then, would hopefully correct whatever might have been missed.

Let me say right here that the day may come when my memory flags where other camp and people facts are concerned, but the sight, smell and sound of an oil-fired furnace will remain clear and vivid until my last breath.

Exactly how many of these monsters I actually checked and inspected over those 26 months during construction days could probably be fairly accurately estimated. I did count up at one stage fairly early on and it was up in the hundreds of thousands. So, no doubt, the total overall would be well over 1,000,000.

It maybe that I hold the distinction of being the only ex-guard who retired with what I call (totally without medical diagnosis, I might add) "furnace thumb" as my right thumb has a distinct lump at the first joint, which I can verify as having been formed because of the thousands of furnace doors I pried open with that particular digital member.

On Road Patrol

While patrolling the barracks and camp area gave you a close view of the residents – and all those furnaces – the time spent on road patrol and traffic checks gave you a completely different perspective and offered a glimpse of the natural wonders of this strange and very different place where we were living. My roommate Jean once remarked that walking your rounds inside camp gave you "tunnel vision" with nothing to see but a bunch of identical white buildings. But when you went on road patrol your eyes were opened to this unusual Arctic landscape of ours. And you got the chance from time to time to glimpse some of its wild inhabitants.

Not that such duty was always pleasant. To give you an example I refer to my journal for a description of my very first road check assignment just after I got to Galbraith in April:

> This is a real Arctic evening – with the wind blowing like hell until you can barely see the road. It's really bitchy! Right here the road is blown bare so even if the snow drifts, you can see some black; but just before coming here, I went up a road that was all snow – real white-out conditions. Hope I get the old pickup back in one piece. The only good thing is that the temperature is not really low. Something like 15 or so;

otherwise, it would be nearly unbearable.

A sort of side consideration is that I've discovered the brakes on this thing are none too good. I tried to stop at the airport but sailed right down the road.

Sure wish you could see this place tonight – it's wild and wooly beyond belief. The wind is so strong it bounces the pickup up and down. It's quite a feat to take my clipboard and sheet out in this and ask questions. Often I can hardly shut the car door.

I have the car faced toward camp which is about four miles away. Sometimes the road ahead is completely obliterated and when a car or truck goes in you see it far ahead as a small black object crawling through the storm.

The time now is 8:00 p.m. I'm quite comfortable inside the pickup with the motor running and the heater going. It's only bad when I see a vehicle approaching and have to get out in the wind. But I've only had six cars so far and doubt if there will be a great number.

A complication could arise if I had to take a pee – am not sure I could get my clothes back in place!

That's a view of the down side of the road patrol. But there was also an up side. The very next month when I went with Roger to meet an incoming plane and set up the road block, the weather was superb. – very scenic and spectacular. We reset the road block at 10:30 p.m. By 11:00 p.m. there was still daylight with a light glow all across the northern horizon. It'll be just another month until the midnight sun is visible. Long banks of fog curl around the mountain shanks from the airport on south. Fog makes for a peculiar atmosphere here – it looks coastal but we are almost 140 miles from the coast.

One of the long-time camp residents told me fog is a harbinger of summer. It occurs often here – socks in planes, and you have to go to Toolik to take off. The fog also creates an odd feeling to air – it must be the dampness. It's very stimulating and pleasant, though cold.

By 11:10 the fog bank expands, lifting to cover the mountains and starts creeping up the valley. It does not move visibly but comes closer steadily. A thin streamer hangs over the lake area, another curls around mountains to the left, getting closer. It's also moving in from the north, so I am on an island with an almost solid circle of fog around, The camp is obscured. . .

That's one type of the interesting weather here, but other evenings are as clear as crystal and it seems you can see forever out over the tundra. Those are the times you are likely to spot the wild inhabitants. The ones you are most likely to see at any time of the year are those great black birds, the Northern Ravens. Almost as often you will probably spot an Arctic Fox or two. In fact, it almost seems at times as if the foxes and the ravens are working together, with the fox finding something good to eat and the ravens cleaning up the scraps.

Other small inhabitants such as the ground squirrels and lemmings are pretty often in view. The larger mammals are not spotted as often, but at times I have seen wolves and caribou and even a grizzly or two while on road patrol.

While I am on the subject of wildlife, large and small, I should mention that we also have quite a few wild visitors – and even a few residents. Just the other day I was reminded of the fact that there are ground squirrels living in camp. I was running down the steps of a barracks and just missed stepping on a squirrel that was sitting there peering up at me. Oh, what a close call.

The larger animals aren't camp residents, although it seems like some of them would like to be. They wander in apparently just curious, or in the case of the bears, drawn by the smell of possible food. I've seen wolves near or actually in camp, some caribou pass nearby. I have never seen moose in the area (although the helicopter pilots say they see a number of them near camp) but the most prominent four-legged camp visitors, are the grizzly bears that come in.

But back to that April road check when I was battling the cold and the wind. Despite the weather, it turned into a busy evening. In four hours, I broke all records for the number of cars logged. Why it was so busy none of us knew. At that time – before a camp gate was in place – we had only a primitive method operating and with vehicles coming in both directions, I had a devil of a time trying to stop them. Then, of course, the majority of people were put out because they had to stop and answer questions, and I had to spend extra time trying to smooth things over.

The point of all this work and time on road checks is to try to stop the rip-offs of company property. But at times it all does seem sort of futile since the thieves have so many other ways to operate.

Chapter 10

The Bear Facts

There is just one animal in the Arctic that deserves a chapter of his own in any book that might be written about pipeline camp life. To say that the Grizzly Bear made day-to-day life for Security Guards interesting – and exciting at times – is an understatement. Brother Bear was really the life of the party, particularly for those guards on the night shifts. He wasn't usually around in the middle of the day, being mainly a nocturnal animal. Come the evening, though, you could often find him trying to sneak into camp.

I got so intrigued by the bear in my early days at Galbraith that I spent some time talking with the Wildlife people and learned some facts I didn't know despite all my years in Alaska. They said the males, which are larger, will run up to 800 to 900 pounds. While they den up in the coldest months, they are not true hibernators and could become active at any time. They are omnivorous and will eat just about anything that smells good. And they are equipped with a sensitive nose to smell out that food.

From watching the bears trying to sneak into camp, I could see they had a very distinctive look and walk. Unlike his smaller cousin the black bear, he has a pronounced hump on his back and a sort of shambling gait. But don't let the looks fool you, it is said he can run as fast as a race horse and he could certainly outrun you or me. He's not an animal you want to tease or harass, but the camp residents were guilty of just such antics more than once and the guards weren't always innocent either.

My own first encounter with Griz came in June when I had been at Galbraith for only a couple of months. He had been reported in camp a couple of times earlier but I missed the action. This night he was back again and really playing games with Roger and Warren. He had a ball sneaking into camp and doing his little jobs up and down the streets between the barracks. Nobody could keep up with him – he really had the men running. He'd grab a few bites of garbage and then hightail it for just outside the camp limits.

He'd rest out there for a bit and then do it all over again. I was walking toward the messhall and there he was clambering into one of the wooden trash bins (something like dumpsters), which had been left with the top up. I called Roger who soon came tumbling out of the messhall in mad chase, but the bear was faster and the last I saw of him he was streaking off with Roger in hot pursuit on foot and Warren bringing up the rear in the Lieutenant's yellow pickup. It was just like the Keystone Cops. But that bear isn't joking, he means business. He found a Suburban that smelled like food – old lunch sacks and probably a few sandwiches inside. With one swipe of his paw he sheared the glass out of a window, crawled inside and really had a ball snooping for goodies.

It's going to be hard to break him of this and send him back to eating ground squirrels and roots. The wildlife people should do it soon because it's becoming a little ridiculous and even dangerous. They could fly him out a good number of miles and he might never be back.

Just five days later the bear was back. Roger got a call from the airport that the bear was at the gravel pit and really giving the crusher crew fits. Roger bear-sat out there for awhile and the bear left – on his way to camp, of course. He was next seen at the outside trash bin. When he couldn't get in, he simply took his paw and ripped off a board. Then he grabbed a sack of garbage and took off. Bud, the bullcook, was standing on a little porch at the edge of camp and he said the bear ran past him, not two feet away. I know this was true because I saw the little trail of manure he left.

Later on, when I was in the shop area, I saw him down beyond the fuel storage among some parked cars. I called Roger again, and by that time he was ambling (the bear I mean) up toward the center of camp. Those things can really move fast. He went by the Sewage Treatment Plant where the big double doors were wide open. I thought sure he'd go in there. Later I talked to Paul there and told him he should keep his doors closed. He said he had the funniest feeling about that time that the bear might come in.

So many doors are left open at night that I get provoked at people. They just don't care or stop to think what's going to happen to a guard if he goes into a supposedly empty building and the bear confronts him.

Anyway, I now approach all empty buildings having open doors with extreme caution. That bear almost ran over Warren when they were chasing him away from the messhall. Roger was after him in the pickup and Pete in the fire truck. And there was old Warren on foot with the bear actually behind him. I saw Warren from a distance (just his head and shoulders) and he was going so fast it looked like he was riding a bicycle. I actually thought, where did Warren get a bicycle?

During our next episode I really got burned up at the male guards. The bear came back into camp about supper time or a little earlier. I got the call and tried to contact Roger, but he was not available. Then I made the mistake of turning the matter over to Warren and Ric. Boy, that was a real mistake – they took off like a couple of hounds chasing a rabbit – very nearly hysterical. Why I turned it over to them I do not know. In mulling it over in my mind, I think it was another of those reflex actions because of being a woman and brainwashed to think that there are certain things men should take care of. This is one attitude I am going to start really fighting. I could herd that bear around just as good as those little bastards – probably even better. I've got to start sticking up for myself because, sure as hell, no one else will.

I soon regretted bitterly bringing those two into it because they simply took over. They left off their furnace checking and made bear-chasing their full-time jobs.

Roger called me around midnight and told me I should guard the bear, taking over from Ric at 12:30. You should have heard the instructions I got from Ric when he reluctantly handed over the pickup to me. "Yes Ric, I know. I know" I've been around bears at least twice as much as he has.

So then the bear went down the creek and out of sight, doubling back to the messhall. By a stroke of good fortune, a very nice guy I know drove around and told me, so I drove toward the messhall, but the bear rushed right by me, poor fellow – he had his mouth open panting like a dog. Then Warren came on the scene, simply hysterical (thinking of course about the ineptness of a woman who let the bear back into camp), calling Roger and telling him to come on because the bear was back in camp. I said very calmly, "Roger, everything is fine. I have everything under control and will look after the bear."

That was exactly true. The bear rushed just outside the camp limits and flopped down like a little kid that's run too far. That was where he rolled over and flopped around with all four feet in the air. What a clown. Then he laid there with his head on his front paws looking at that lousy yellow pickup that chased him when he got up. He must have stayed in that same spot for half an hour, then got up and started around the perimeter, trying to sneak across the line every few yards. I stayed very close ,so he kept on until he got to the dump. This was where he saw a fox, stood up on his hind legs to get a better look and then took off in that deceptive, lumbering lope that a bear has and chased the fox clear out of sight. Roger soon came to take over.

I hope I got a photo or two of the bear – I was using the telephoto and just opened it up. This was my night in the shop area and I got a number of interesting shots. There were a couple of caribou lying down and I sneaked up on them, taking them while in repose with their beautiful horns standing up straight, and then again when they stood up to look at me.

After this bear episode, things were quiet for awhile and I also left the scene to go on R & R. But then, about the middle of August, things got really lively when the bear returned. He came back about midnight and stayed around longer than ever before. Until about noon, I think. From what I heard, a crowd of people gathered out at the edge of camp to take photos just like they were visiting the zoo. I guess the day guards had a real hard time keeping things under control and were never successful in keeping the people away.

People can be so foolish: These are *not* tame animals. But then the guards are not always above reproach either. One of the shop men told me he saw Ric standing up on a little hill throwing rocks at the bear. As fast as those bears can move, he could have been on Ric in no time if he had felt mean.

This time of year with winter almost upon us, and cave time approaching, the bears are hard put to find as much last-minute food as they can. That means they are not always in the sweetest of moods. I sure hope no one gets hurt before this bear goes away.

Our next grizzly was a newcomer and a youngster. He was a golden grizzly that lurked around the pumphouse for several days before deciding he would try getting into camp. That night I got a good look at him and he appeared to be a two-year-old and probably just kicked out by his mother. He tried all night to get into camp, no doubt smelling the enticing food aromas. But Eric patrolled the edges with a shovel and also fired a shotgun to scare him.

That bear looked like just a ball of fur. His legs and underside were a deep brown, while his back and head were golden. Poor bear, he tried and tried to run the blockade. Meanwhile, people were doing all sorts of foolish things like going after him across the tundra in a pickup. Once, they cornered him between buildings. Again it's a wonder someone didn't get hurt.

THE NIGHT OF THE BIG PARTY proved even more exciting. This was a Saturday night and there was an Alyeska-sanctioned party with people from all the surrounding camps – Toolik, Pump 4 and so on, arriving at Galbraith by the bus loads. So we had the bear and all those drunks at the same time. It was really something.

There was a big dance, a talent show and live music. The bear came early. He was in camp by 6:00 p.m. I went over to the messhall about 10 minutes later and Ric and Roger were already there. The bear had been holing up under the messhall where it must have smelled awfully good to him. All we could do is park the pickups near the holes and wait for him to take his own sweet time in coming out. That night it took five hours to get him out of the center of camp. I never moved out of my pickup from 6:10 until after 11:00 p.m.

By 8 o'clock, crowds and hordes of drunks were milling around and they were all interested in the bear. In fact, I have never seen so many bear experts in all my borned days. Nine-tenths of these people are from Tulsa and places like that and have never even seen a bear before so how they became experts I'll never know. It was just simply disgusting. I have come to loathe even more a southern accent – it was all just a mess.

Ric was on one side of the messhall with one pickup and I on the other. If the crowd had just let us alone we could have gotten the bear out in good time.

Several times he started to come out. One time that I was witness to, he came out and all these people crowded in on him so that he had not a place to run – so he went up to the place that had been boarded up where he had formerly gone under the building, and with one swipe of a paw he tore up the boards and dived underneath. Poor bear. Once when he was tearing around a corner, a girl bullcook was standing just around the corner with her back to it and the bear actually passed between her and the building, not more than two or three feet from her. We screamed at her and she turned just in time to see the bear disappear. She crossed herself.

While this was going on, Roger was awfully busy patrolling the arctic walkway and trying to keep some order at the dance. Many of the people came in the big buses, and there were several of these. Once Roger had to talk to one of the drivers, and he said later that pot smoke was so thick in that bus that he almost choked. (I'm sure he is a pot smoker himself, so he really knows).

So pot and booze were flowing freely. The people were jammed in the new messhall where the party was held, just like sardines. From seeing a great number of the people who attended, I would say that it was the rowdier element of the camps. (This covers a wide portion of the population, I'll grant you.) I really wasn't favora-

Wilma (L) and her sister,

Wilma, Bette and their mother,
Cricket

Riverside High School Class of 1937
Wilma is seated second from left.

Wilma the cowgirl

Collecting snow for water in
Anchorage after the 1964 earthquake

Camping in a beached schooner at
Tuktoyaktuk on the Arctic Ocean

Wilma with Helen Coolidge (R)

In her room at Happy Valley

With Henri, the cook at
Summit Station

Inside the pipe

With Dick north and camera gear on
The Great Re-badging Expedition

In her organic garden

Ladies' barracks, Galbraith Camp

Wilma and Bob at the cabin at Willow

Millie Saunders, Wilma's niece

Wilma on patrol at the YukonRiver Bridge

The E.L. Patton, Yukon River Bridge - Laurel Sliney

Jean Layman, Wilma's roommate (Left)

Andrea from Culinary (Right) at Galbraith

Ray Leach at Galbraith

Do Not Disturb sign

A long, long, hallway

Unidentified Lady Truck Driver,
Galbraith

Dick North taking care of the bear (R)

An unidentified "Pipeliner"

Guard Robert McCoy
checks furnace on fire watch

"Largest Cat House North of the Arctic Circle!" Galbraith

Fire truck at Happy Valley airport

"Do not cut this tree, farthest north White Spruce on pipeline corridor"

Galbraith Camp

bly impressed. I have a feeling this may end the parties for awhile.

Well the night of that big party was the very last time I ever saw that bear. Not that he disappeared, but just after that, my long-awaited transfer came through. After some six months at Galbraith I was being moved on north to a new camp.

THE HAPPY VALLEY CAMP was something completely new and different for me. It was a different camp, with new people to meet, and the country was completely different. Where Galbraith was set in a bowl with mountains all around, Happy Valley was right out there on the flat tundra. We were now some 60 miles on north and that much closer to Prudhoe and the Arctic Ocean.

So everything at Happy was just completely new and different for me except for one thing: Bears! The bear situation appeared to be even worse than at Galbraith. There were three different bears that rambled around camp at night. We haven't the manpower to actually patrol for them and it would do little good anyway. The only thing you do is chase them from Camp A over the hill and across the road to Camp B. Then when you go to B, it chases them back to A.

Just to make things more interesting, there are two or three wolves that also make forays into camp. Between the bears and the wolves and having to tromp around outside in the mud, life never gets dull. There are six or eight barracks that are not connected with walkways and you have to go outside to check them. So out we go in the dark with nothing more than a flashlight to guide our way and protect us. I don't like this situation even a little bit.

Here it is mid-October and full winter weather, and at least one of our bears is still around. I was on roving patrol about two this morning, when I drove up and surprised him licking out a garbage can. He took off running like mad and went as far as a little ravine where he dived over the edge. Then he stood there looking into my spotlight with his eyes gleaming like green lamps. In a few minutes I turned off the light, then turned it on again, and he was already sneaking back. The spotlight actually scares him off–he can't stand it for long.

Even though its really winter here this far North, I continue to see other animals. A few caribou are someplace around, though we seldom see them at night. Most amazing of all, a moose or two has wandered by. I just couldn't believe they came this far North. This tree-less tundra is such a poor place for moose, yet they are here.

The ground squirrels have long since gone to bed. The ravens are here and even a few gulls. I just can't imagine that the gulls stay all winter, but this sure looks like it. The only other things I see are teensy little mice or shrews running through the snow in the car headlights. Imagine such tiny creatures living in this cold and snow. Some look not more than two inches long.

This Arctic region is an amazing and interesting place. Even with its long, long winters and its terrific sub-zero temperatures and punishing winds, it still manages to support a healthy and amazingly varied population of animal and bird life.

The Arctic Weather & Landscape

Whenever I'm off the job and out in civilization talking with "civilians," the first question they always ask is something about the Arctic cold during the long, dark winters. Then the second question, of course, will be something like "How in the world can you stand to live and work under such conditions?" Then I try to give them an extra shiver or two by mentioning the fact that one of our camps, where I have worked (Atigun), holds the United States all-time record for low temperature at minus 80 degrees.

What I try to explain to these folks is that the Native residents of the Arctic have managed to live there, and in relative comfort, for thousands of years. And that we, the outsiders, can learn to adapt to the cold if we come equipped with all of the clothing and equipment to also live in relative comfort. The fact is that once you get down in the sub-zero temperatures it really doesn't make all that much difference whether it's 40 below or 60 below. You just have to plan for it and take the obvious precautions.

If I have the time, I go on to say that in my opinion the long, dark winters are more than made up for by our short but glorious summers. In my four years in the Arctic, I came to really cherish the unique conditions with the long, long daylight hours in the summer – the Midnight Sun – and the splendid display of wildflowers across the green tundra with the still-snowy mountains in the background.

When I first arrived in the Arctic in mid-April, I really didn't know what to make of the weather this far North. My journal recorded "a grey day in Galbraith." I described the weather as quite strange, with many of the characteristics of alpine country, which it really is – Arctic Alpine. That night, after all the wind went down, it was quite nice. I was running around without my parka – and what a sensation! I felt as light and free as a bird.

Then, all of a sudden, almost in the space of 15 minutes, the temperature dropped 23 degrees, and there we were below zero again! We weren't really in the springtime yet. We were still on the outer edge of our long winter. When dawn broke, clouds were hanging low and it all looked very stormy. I said at the time that I found the Arctic weather most interesting and looked forward to what it's like in what passes for summer here. While it may get hot at times – up to 90 or more – I felt sure there would be a wild variety of temperatures. Old-timers at Galbraith told me it can and does snow in the summer. One person commented: "There's two seasons here, winter and the Fourth of July. And it can snow on the Fourth!"

I decided to adopt a wait-and-see attitude and be ready for anything. The rest of April brought nights of enormous beauty, as the spring fog shrouded the camp and transformed every object in it. I saw a thousand possible photos and hoped that I could remember all of them: The giant frosted fuel bladders, buildings crusted with icy rime, snow-splotched hills wrapped in fog, ravens all puffed-up and damp, big machinery, propane tanks in different colors, the fence with frosted barbs. Tiny crystals fall continually; bigger than the ice fog we know and the crystals themselves feel barbed.

BY THE TIME MAY HAD ARRIVED, things were definitely changing. This one day I remember arrived sunny and hazy with a real feeling of warmth in the air. The snow was going fast and on the heels of this slight change in season, we started to see the first arriving song-birds. For me, the first place honors went to a white-crowned sparrow. Eric spotted the first robin.

After the lengthy sunset, I watched the moon going down between two mountains. The moon and the mountains were the same pale, thin shade of translucent white. It appeared that the moon sat on the mountain's lap. Quite a sight! More and more these sunsets were beginning to look like the Midnight Sun. At one point on my rounds, the very low sun shone into the tiny window of the back door of X Barracks and made the hallway floor shimmer – a small but memorable spot of beauty in the unfinished, drab barracks. This happens each night now.

On May 10, we got our first really warm day – it got up to 52 degrees in the shade at Galbraith; back in Fairbanks it climbed to 82. It was simply flawless weather here. To be able to work outside in it was perfect. Not so perfect was the first mosquito that I saw and killed – the first of what they say will be hordes to come. A day later, I saw a miller moth and the first fly.

I should mention also, that the next day was Mothers' Day and, in honor of it, the chefs fixed a special display of salads, molded and garnished to the nth degree. It had Rene's special bread basket as the centerpiece – a really beautiful table. When I went in for chow, I had to dash back to my room for the camera. I took 10 shots of the table, plus John and Tom, the chefs. The main dish was delicious roast beef – the best since I'd been there.

A few days later, I began to wonder if spring had really arrived after all. The night was cold, foggy and unpleasant. Then, after a good sleep, I got up at 2:00 p.m., looked out the window, and by God it was snowing! Despite that, a whole flock of screaming seagulls arrived back for the summer. So, winter or summer, make your guess and take your chances.

THEN JUNE ARRIVED AND WE really were starting to see our brief but wonderful summer. One early June day, I awoke to a nice partly-sunny sky. This country has such a nice, washed look at this time. The surrounding mountains were pale grey and there were no trees to clutter up the landscape. A truly gorgeous sight. I sort of goofed off, feeling lazy, and just enjoyed a half hour out at the dynamite shack where there is no noise except the sound of a nice creek coming down from the hills and the call of birds. My day was enriched by the sight of about five of the barren ground caribou grazing off in the distance.

The very next day when I got up, it was shiny bright outside, and I really scurried around getting ready and took off to take pictures. The bears are seldom around in the daytime, so I walked up the hill across the creek and took a number of shots of the camp, of Pump station 4 and all around.

That area was just covered with wildflowers, and they were just astounding. There were just so many varieties. The ground cover of White Mountain Aviens was still there but some are fading and larger plants – but not much higher – are coming in. One is the dwarf fireweed and up here it really is dwarf.

I only wish everyone who thinks the Arctic is a barren wasteland could see how beautiful the tundra is. The ground was just exactly like a carpet, a real mass of small but colorful, low flowers. I never saw anything more lovely. You can't really see them from a distance, but they're so pretty as you walk across the tundra. I couldn't see that we were due to have very many taller flowers, but these little ones in a solid mass are very effective.

A bit later in the summer, one day in July was worth remembering. The day before all we had was rain and mosquitoes. It's hard to think of having them at the same time, but there they were. On my shift there was nothing else to think about – extremely dead and dull. Not even a good rousing drunk to enliven the evening.

But then in the wee hours of the morning everything changed, and it became so beautiful. The rain and clouds cleared and everything was sparkling clean. For a few hours the mosquitoes seemed to go away too, so every time I came out of a building I stopped to admire the beauty of the whole landscape. I think I shall always remember this place as one of the most gorgeous I have ever seen, despite the cold and the mosquitoes.

While there were beautiful summer days to re-member, there were also storms, and on a later July day I woke at 2:00 p.m. to one of them. It was pouring rain when I got up, but even that seemed pleasant. In fact, I'll always remember that rain at Galbraith was quite pleas-ant because it sounded so soothing pattering on the roofs of these metal barracks. It's no wonder the tundra is so green at this time of year. I remember thinking that the rocky mountain in the distance may even turn green be-fore this is over.

Just a couple of weeks later on August 8th, I re-corded the first signs that our wonderful but brief sum-mer was starting to come to an end. The day started out with snow coming down like mad. Then it turned into a gorgeous summer-fall day with the sun shining, fluffy clouds dotting the sky, and no snow visible except on the mountain tops. There was a hint of fall in the air, but it was just a delightful day.

That was just about my last glimpse of summer. In September I was transferred from Galbriath to a more northern camp at Happy Valley. The season was more advanced there and the green tundra had turned to a deep red-brown with sort of a yellow tint – different but still beautiful.

Chapter 12

On to Happy Valley

"Well, here I am all settled in at Happy Valley, Camp A, roughly 75 miles on north from Galbraith. This is certainly a different kind of camp and even a different type of country." That's the way I started my letters to family and friends early in September of 1975. It was a true enough statement, although it probably didn't get across just *how* different things really were.

First of all, there was a different attitude about the residents and the security guards. Also there were two Happy Valley camps, and they were each different from the other. There was both a new camp and an older one. I was located in the older Camp A. The new part, Camp B, was less than a quarter-mile away, but you couldn't see it because we were located in a swale. Actually, B had a much nicer location because it was on a flat section of land so you could see out over the tundra and there was a river nearby. From Camp B on a very clear day, you could see in the far, far distance the snowy peaks of the Brooks Range.

Supposedly, the story goes that one of the first surveyors helping set up the first camp looked around and said something like: "Well, this looks like a happy valley!" They say that's how the camp got its name. Perhaps. But like I mentioned earlier, this old camp really isn't located in a valley, it's just a little swale – sort of a dip in the rolls.

Unlike Galbraith, which is just about encircled by mountains, Happy is set out in the tundra. But because of the swale it's the most closed-in place I have ever seen. A very odd place to say the least.

NANA has an office in Camp A and another in Camp B. When I first got to Happy, I was put on nights again, and my 12-hour shift was rotated over 4-hour stretches in both camps. I really liked the people I worked with there – they were all very nice. (Probably the people in the last camp were just as nice, but after six months or more in a camp you get jaded and you need to get out and see new faces and meet some new people.)

There is a darling young Eskimo boy of 21 or so, who is one of the nicest people imaginable. He is so handsome and intelligent and a very gentle type of person. His ambition is to be a minister and go back to his village to help his people. He is a member of the Friends Church. There is also another Eskimo man on nights, a bit older but a rather grumpy, red-haired young man who actually is very nice and helpful despite the fact that he is grumpy. I get along with everyone and like them.

There is a completely different atmosphere here at Happy than at Galbraith. I don't know whether I mentioned it or not, but Galbraith was a sort of headquarters for at least the northern section of the pipeline, so it was often full of "big wheels." The feeling there was sometimes a bit strained; but at Happy we're so much more relaxed. There are some "wheels" here too, but you can't tell them from the other people. Another thing I like a lot is that the meal hours are longer and I no longer have to wolf my food. I can go to dinner and relax and really en-joy it. And all the things I heard about Happy having such wonderful food are really true. It's simply over-whelming the amount of food and the variety that is accessible day and night.

Perhaps the biggest drawback – if you can call it that – to Happy, in comparison to Galbraith, is that it is not nearly so nicely kept and clean. Galbraith was just immaculate, and all painted and carpeted. Gravel walks were strung between the buildings so that even in spring breakup you never had to walk in mud. Well, Happy has a lot of unpainted arctic walkways and we wade through mud between buildings. Nothing is quite as clean.

Another negative factor is that we have the 798ers here. The 798 is the union of the Pipeliners (These are the men from Tennessee, Texas and other southern states who actually weld the pipe.) Their being here means it is a more noisy and troublesome camp.

But I made up my mind that no matter where I went, I would find it interesting and likable and so I honestly do like Happy and find it most enjoyable just because of its differences. I am the only woman guard here, so I'm rooming with a camp worker – in this case a young thing who has worked as a laborer. Our working and off hours don't mesh as smoothly as two opposite shift guards would, but there again, I promised myself that no matter what I encountered I would make it work.

All that said, I still have to admit that no matter how you slice it, this sort of life is not the best – you don't really have any life of your own. Now that I have a different set-up as far as roommates are concerned, I have less privacy than ever. However, I will muddle through some way and when I am all through working, I'm going off someplace and really relax for a long, long time. God knows when that will be.

Then there are the difficulties of the job itself. The other night it was really cold for September, and I had to wear my heavy parka even in the truck. Then the pickup broke down while I was out on patrol and I had to wait and wait before anyone could come out to rescue me. I doubt that the temperature was much below zero but there was a strong wind, which brought the chill factor down.

One thing of interest is that there is far less "control" over telephone calls here than at Galbraith. That is a good feature, because it's nice to be able to call family and friends once in awhile, rather than just having to depend on writing letters.

In fact, everything is more relaxed at Happy. This is odd too because our captain more or less makes this his headquarters and I see far more of him than ever before. But he seems less fearful or up-tight, if you want to put it that way, than before. He was on the plane coming up from Fairbanks and we talked all the way, so I think I understand him better now. He's really a decent sort and we tend to to get along fine. Probably my attitude has changed also since I no longer hold any of the NANA brass in awe. If anything, Captain Carr and I might see eye-to-eye more than with some of the guards, simply because we're more the same age.

I have to mention that it seems to me that this camp has been arranged rather oddly. Each side has an arctic walkway and the barracks and all other living-space buildings; messhalls, rec rooms and so on, are along the walkway as well. In Camp A we actually have to walk across a small area between two sets of buildings. But my barracks, N, is along a walkway so I don't even have to go outside to go to work. When I get up and get going for the day, I can just walk down to our Camp A office and get coffee before starting work. That seems a bit odd.

CAMP B IS WHERE all the excitement is. That's where the 798 Pipeliners are housed and there is plenty of excitement over there. For several hours after I went to work at 6:00 p.m. there was a steady flow of fire alarms (nearly all false), complaints about various things, people trying to get housing and other odds and ends. The two guards arc run ragged for a short time, but I like it. I wish it would be like that for the entire shift – or at least half of it. It's a real challenge.

I am more or less studying Pipeliners at the moment, being associated with them as closely as this. The other craft union members seem to hate them and always give them a bad name. I've heard such fearful stories about them – what a rotten bunch they are – that it's interesting to be able to draw my own conclusions. While I am repelled by their talk and attitude in general, I cannot honestly say that I have found them any worse than anyone else here. Personally, I've been treated with undeviating respect. That's funny too, in view of their attitude toward "broads" and "niggers." Whether you can lump all these men together is as questionable in my mind, as whether you can lump any other group together.

Captain Carr and some of the other NANA officials have expounded at length as to what they see as the Pipeliners' psychology and a lot of the things they pointed out made sense. For instance, great numbers of these men are actually related in one way or another, either by blood or marriage. They tend to come from very poor areas, and many in the past were considered "poor white trash." In many ways this seems to account for their attitude toward women and blacks: Everyone has to have someone they consider lower than themselves.

I have learned that Crabtree is the big name in the Pipeliner group. There are dozens of Crabtrees and near relations of Crabtrees here. One whole barracks here is hardly anything other than Crabtrees.

The head of this clan appears to be a man who goes by the name of Smokey Crabtree, who lives back in the tiny town of Fouke, Arkansas. This man wrote a book called *Smokey and the Monster*, which is being sold here for $5 by his brother who is a member of the Pipeliner group. There is a lot of Pipeliner philosophy and psychology in this book (which the guy published himself), according to other people. So I had to buy a copy. It's only interesting if you're trying to get a line on the Pipeliners. From that standpoint it is quite fascinating.

Late in September I fell ill, a bad cold or the flu or something. I wrote in my journal that September 27th was the first day that I felt well enough to get the typewriter out and make notes. The day before, I felt so rotten that I asked the sergeant not to give me outside patrol. I just could not face going out in the cold to drive. That was the day I received in the mail a humidifier and a heating pad and slept with them both on. They helped but still I do not feel as well as I should. I wonder if my health will be the thing that will make me give up this pipeline job. I felt so good the first two tours, but this third one has been different.

Anyway, that first day back on outside patrol I saw something that grew into a continuing strange episode. You could call it the case of the truck thief who never seemed to get anyplace.

IN THE FIRST ACT the truck thief stole one of the large pipe-hauling trucks. I actually saw the first theft take place but had no idea it really was a theft. It happened about 6:30 or 7:00 p.m. I saw this young man, who had a woman with him, run over to this big truck that was idling by the side of the road. They got in and it started moving. He seemed to be a bit inept in driving a big rig but not so much that anyone would have thought much of it. Why he chose a big truck I'll never know; there are so many pickups just sitting around.

This first truck he stole, he just ran it a little way, then ran into a ditch. A few hours later he stole a second one and ran it closer to Franklin. The next day I heard that he stole a pickup and drove back to Happy where he rammed the pickup into the side of another parked long-haul truck – not once but *twice!* After that he simply got out and left and he is still at large. They think he must have at least a black eye out of the ramming episodes, so we've been told to watch for any men with bruised faces

Who is this young man and how does he have enough time to be driving around in stolen trucks? I have a theory that there's a considerable number of "floaters" living in these camps, not just at Happy but also elsewhere. However, Happy would be especially adaptable to their needs because of the two camps. I know of at least one man who was apparently not working and was a very mysterious character. We saw him at odd times of the day or night, just wandering around, sleeping in the rec rooms or theaters, though on the roster he was legitimate.

It is my theory that he did, perhaps, work here for awhile, and then either quit or was terminated, and after that just stayed on. It's a perfect place for that. With all the thousands of employees, and all the coming and going, you just know that the paper records are a mess and often way out of date. So, even without a job, it is just a perfect place for a loafer: warm places to sleep and three or more good free meals a day, plus free movies, reading material, even companionship. You don't need a dime in your pocket. Everything is free: free showers and laundry service. What more do you need?

While you are supposedly manifested in and out, there must be ways of just stopping off in another camp. One woman we know of did just that.

She was terminated at Franklin and promptly got off the plane at Happy and got herself another job. What a nut she was. She was really homicidal and suicidal, and the last few days before she was finally thrown out of Happy, she went prowling around the walkways and barracks having hysterics and just raising hell in general. We ran afoul of each other several times and each time was a real experience. She was living with a 798er at the last.

In October things seemed to quiet down. With the colder temperatures arriving, our bears were seen less and less often, and even the human inhabitants of camp seemed to get less playful. About the same time ,we got two men and I wasn't impressed with either. One had been an MP and the other a policeman for five years. They both think they're big shots and the ex-policeman figures he is above furnace checking. He does all he can to get out of it. He spent four hours last night making out a 15-minute report while I checked furnaces. The other one likes to play detective. He cooks up all these elaborate and wild schemes to trap people and just ignores the job he's really here for, which is to keep a close fire watch. Unfortunately the sergeant we have right now is sort of an aesthetic type and hardly a match for these two.

We have people coming out of our ears right now — just when we are getting into the slow winter season. Our new sergeant will arrive in a couple of days (I'm glad of that.), which will bring us up to nine guards. And the captain is bringing back a new lieutenant, which means an extra one over what we had. This whole thing is always in a state of flux with people coming and going and new rules and regulations.

I just try to live from day to day, never knowing how long the job will last. One thing I must do is not to imagine it can't end at any time. I try not to look ahead and think about things we want it to do for us. The only thing I can do is to keep socking the money into the bank or credit union and hope we end up with enough to do us some good.

By mid-October we were having some dreary days at Happy Valley. With the little skift of snow on the ground and the overcast skies, it's sort of depressing. This what you rather expect the Arctic to be like – *harsh.* But it was beautiful the other night when I was on outside patrol. The moon was out and big and bright and you could see the whole valley. I now drive out to the dynamite storage places about a couple of miles outside of camp. There is a solid waste burn pit out near there too. Sometimes you see the bears out there, and others have seen wolves and foxes there. The last time I saw the bigger bear. He doesn't appear to be that afraid of the pickup, though the light annoys him some. He lopes off for a short distance and when you turn the lights off he comes right back. Sure wish I could see some wolves out there. Everyone has seen them but me.

THE NEXT DAY, AMAZINGLY ENOUGH, was just like summer. At the same time there were tremendous storms both north and south of us. It was 101 below (with the chill factor) at Prudhoe. Here at Happy our temperature went up to 15 above, and I was able to shed the parka for the down vest. It was a nice clear day too, but I had the feeling that it was just the lull before the storm hits us.

One thing I wanted to mention is the appearance of the ravens around here. No matter how cold it has gotten, there always seems to be quite a number of them that hang around for the scraps they can scrounge. They have

the strangest appearance, especially when the temperature is low. Sometimes they just sit right out in the snow.
You'll see these black things sitting in the snow like gulls
on the water. You wonder just what they are because the
country is very flat and white, and then you get closer
and see it's the ravens. They puff up their feathers, and,
if it's very cold, their head feathers frost up just like a
man's whiskers. In fact, they do remind me very much of
little old black men with grey whiskers.

With just the much-reduced winter crew here, we
locked up B Camp on December 8. Despite that though,
I have the feeling that a few people are managing to live
in there. On my last round through the barracks, I
opened a few doors just to check the rooms and in what
had been the women's barracks, the last room was definitely still occupied. The whole thing was supposed to
have been empty but, quite often I fear, there are little
deals in a situation of this kind. Just one person left inside could open a door and everything inside loaded onto
trucks. I sure don't trust all of the truck drivers.

About that same time my roommate was leaving
for Minnesota. Sure wish they would forget to give me
another, but suppose that can't possibly happen. I guess I
might as well get used to the idea of someone around all
the time. The woman who is here now is really quite
nice, somewhere in my age group, and easy to get along
with. Her husband is a heavy equipment operator and
has been down in Dietrich. They will be out for the holidays and expect to return when the camp opens again.

That night I was so unhappy when I went to the
post office on the way to dinner and they had changed

hours and it was closed again. They do this frequently, though I think the big reason is because the planes are so erratic. There has been nothing but trouble in the past week because of ice fog in the Fairbanks area. It sure makes travel and mail service a hassle here.

I have been feeling so lonesome recently. Maybe the whole thing is creeping up on me; or it's the thought of the Christmas holiday approaching.

Just then, when things were at their lowest point, something new and different came along and gave me a real boost. This was something that would get me away from the camp and the boring routine for a number of days. It would also give me the opportunity to see the other Arctic camps and do some photo work of a sort. It was what I came to describe as The Great Re-Badging Expedition. It was a whole story in itself and I will skip over it here and describe it at length in a later chapter.

Once I returned from the expedition and the holidays were over, the real winter routine set in. The camp population was at a new low, the work seemed to slow down or stop, and the real cold, cold arrived and made life generally more difficult.

With the camp practically denuded of people and with most of the animals tucked in to wait out the winter, there really wasn't much to do or see. All this really started to affect me, and I started to feel lazy and tired. It even got to be too much of a chore for me to drag out the typewriter and keep up my journal. By the time February rolled around, I had arrived at a solution of sorts. I typed up a form and got it Mimeographed. I thought this was all pretty ingenious.

My form had space for reports for two days. At the top was space for the date and for the temperature (taken daily at 7:00 p.m. while I was on shift). Then came spaces for "Animals I saw," for birds seen, for a summary of the day, and for "thoughts." I compiled these reports faithfully, except for our deep-freeze days in February.

That month really was a deep-freeze. For instance, on February 10th, I recorded a 7:00 p.m. temperature of minus 22. The next day it was 34 below. On February 14th, it was again 34 below. I added a weather note: "Cold, clear. The cold is steady, intense, quiet." On the 21st, it dropped down to 50 below and the following day to minus 55.

That, apparently, was the low point. Then it started warming up a bit. On the 25th, it was minus 35, and on the following day I actually recorded "Above Zero!" Things were on the upswing from then on and our deep freeze was finally thawing. On March 1st, it was plus 5 degrees and by the 7th of the month, it had gotten up to 15 above. It appeared we were finally on the way to spring and our short but glorious summer.

The Great Re-Badging Expedition

The whole story about what I came to describe as The Great Re-Badging Expedition began to unfold just four days before Christmas. One of our guards, Dick North, who had been working at Pump Station 4, was given the word that he had to go on another badge-making tour and starting the very next day. He had done this before and he wasn't at all happy about having to take it on again, particularly over the Christmas holidays. He was really upset.

Without really thinking it over, I offered to learn the job and take it over from him, to spell him off. The lieutenant thought that it was a good idea. In the afternoon, the captain called and said I could do it if I wanted. When I checked in at the office I was set. It seemed exciting, and I broke up housekeeping. I hated to tear up my nice room, but this new job seemed to offer more than just keeping on with my present boring work.

Tried to call Bob, but he was just not talking when I finally got him. I was upset about this, and I also got to thinking that I might be taking a pay cut by taking this new job. I finally had to get up about 1:00 a.m. and went over to the office to check, but they assured me I would still be getting the same pay. All set to go by 7:30 a.m. I called Bob one last time and said I would call again from Fairbanks. The expediter took us to the airport. Dick is

116

going along with me to teach me the ropes. I am not certain how long we'll stay in Fairbanks.

The reason behind this whole re-badging expedition was rather unclear to us down at the peon level. It appears that higher-ups at Alyeska had decided that their present identification badge system was insecure and new IDs were needed. The result was this expedition on which we would photograph every single employee on the northern portion of the pipeline project. There would be nothing artistic about the work. We would be getting "mug shots" using a rather complicated and bulky machine such as they use at the DMV and in coin-photo booths. When we did our work, and the machine did its, the result would be a laminated ID badge. We would do this hundreds and hundreds of times at all the camps and pump stations north of the Yukon. We would first spend some time in Fairbanks getting instructions on operating our machine.

So, here we were on the plane to Fairbanks sitting apart. Dick refused to sit next to me – in a huff?

I have to admit I found Dick North rather an odd duck. I couldn't help but fear that the time we had to spend working together might be rather strained. At times, he appeared friendly enough; at others very reserved and stand-offish. He was rather slight and thin with greying hair and glasses. About 45 to 50 I would guess. He really had the appearance of a college professor rather than a security guard. He was actually a former newspaperman, working for papers in the Lower 48 and then on the *Juneau Daily Empire*. Eventually he moved over to Canada's Yukon Territory, settled in

Whitehorse, and became active as a Northern historian and writer. He had had one historical non-fiction book published: *The Mad Trapper of Rat River,* and I gathered he was researching another.

The weather in Happy Valley when we left was fair and not too cold, about minus 15. The flight to Fairbanks was uneventful. Mary from the commissary and I were the only women on the plane. No friends aboard. Dick and I took a cab out to the Alyeska office at Fort Wainwright – $5 each. We had lunch in the cafeteria and then settled in a fairly nice room in Murphy Hall. I was very tired after practically no sleep the night before. I almost got a roommate but discouraged it. Then went to dinner with Dick. We had to be at the ID place by 7:45 a.m. so I turned in early.

Just before going to bed, I finally was able to get Bob on the phone. He will be up tomorrow. We'll go out to dinner and have a talk. I feel very lonely as if we are drifting apart. But I'm going to try to be cheerful and happy. If I lose Bob, then I lose all that I have been working for.

I'm up early the next morning and ready to go. I walk through a utilidor tunnel to the cafeteria and have breakfast. Then to Building 1040 where I report to the ID Section promptly at 7:45. A young black woman, Pat, and Bryan Miller are there and we work all day badging people. I find it very confusing trying to get everybody with the right insignia and background. Then I am really shocked when we get word that we are to start north by noon and be in Prospect or Five Mile by tonight.

Chapter 13

I was horrified! Now I won't get to see Bob after all. The two people we are working with and Dick all tell me I should call the boss of the project, Bob Koslick and object. I do and he tells me this is a rush, rush job and we must work each site in a matter of hours. He finally relents, and says to take until tomorrow.

I am bitterly sorry now that I took on this job. I can sure see why Dick didn't want it. But I can't get out of it now. I tell Dick I hate it.

I meet this Bob Koslick – he seems reasonable and he asks me to call from time to time and tell him how things are going. Then I go over to Traveler's Inn where Bob Knox has checked in. Bob is relaxed and happy, more like he used to be. We spend a good evening. We have dinner at the Hide-A-Way. It's not really a good dinner but nice because we are having a good time. We get up early and have breakfast at 6:00 a.m. We meet Dick at 7:00 and then Bob leaves for the trip back to Anchorage. Dick and I pack up our machine, take the vehicle to get gas, and then head on north.

As we set out, we drive into a grey day. I had forgotten what the scenery was like, but soon recall the rolling domes and trees. The road is good enough but rough and it winds up and down. We stop at the village of Livengood and have tea at a modest cafe called Sam's. The young man running the place has quite an accent and is a cousin to "Charles DeGaule" a character who bore a striking resemblance to the famous French leader. The "General" ran the Economy Cafe in Fairbanks but now lives here.

We head on north and do not see the Livengood camp. We drive up a long, high hill and enter ice fog. There are some tremendous views of pink, fogged sky with heavily-iced evergreen trees. Simply stunning. We stop on top and I change to color film, It's almost too late, but I do try some shots. Dick sleeps a lot while I drive.

The truth is that Dick is upset about having to go along to teach me the job. He does not want to be traveling with me, and has shown that from the first by refusing to sit beside me on the plane. On this portion of the trip, he had soon told me that he was going to teach me how to drive this snowy road, and that he would sleep, which he did. Although the vehicle was automatic, he said in most spots keep it in second, or at least in places that looked dubious, and not to drive fast. He promptly went to sleep and I drove very successfully, and according to his instructions as I saw fit. (It's all really kind of funny because I've probably driven a hell of a lot more snowy roads than Dick North ever has.)

The only other thing to note about his ire at being along, is that at the very first place he stopped, while he was making arrangements to set up, I hauled in Dick's suitcase to his room, to prove to him that I was not a lady who had to be waited on – in fact, rather than seeking help, I was more than ready to help him. This ploy worked. Dick soon thawed as much as he was going to thaw for me, and we ended the trip having a good deal of fun working together. That was really all I wanted. Dick was not my cup of tea, nor was I his.

We stopped at the checkpoint at the north end of the Yukon River bridge. This bridge is awfully odd. It starts way uphill and slopes down. It's the first "steep" bridge I ever saw. We met the NANA guards and the sergeant. They work Diamond Willow in their spare time – quite nice

We continue on driving slowly – we average about 30 mph – Dick is very fussy about that. Just after dark, somewhere around 4:00 p.m., we pull into Old Man Camp. We arc met by the Alyeska auditor, Steve, to whom I take an instant dislike. He wants to know why we are so late. I tell him we take time driving and stay within the speed limit. I also tell him that, as a sour-dough, I am aware how these roads *should be driven.* We set up equipment and take pictures at once. Quite hectic. We do over 100 in next few hours – in fact, finish. Old Man seems a good camp and I have a room alone, but no time to spend in it. To bed at 10:00 p.m.

The next day proved to be a pretty easy one. I got up at 4:30 a.m., had some breakfast, and then we finished up a few badges. We loaded our equipment, and drove on to Prospect. We set up in an unused messhall and had a leisurely day taking pictures as people dribbled in. I stayed in a 56-man barracks, which was nice but quite chilly. We took a break from 2:00 p.m. until 4:30 and then did 14 more and finished up by 7:00 p.m. We went over to the messhall and had a steak. One odd thing: There are red squirrels here at Prospect and they come into the messhall.

I slept in until 7:00 a.m. the next day. It was December 24 – Christmas Eve – but just another work day.

We finish up a few badges. I shoot some pictures and shoot the breeze. Dick is moping around and acts cool to me. Well, I wouldn't choose him for a companion to be marooned with either!

He has Steve's car to drive to Coldfoot, so I load up the equipment and take off about 11:00 a.m. It is just daylight and a cloudy day. I enter the mountains and go up and down long grades. On the level, the snow is broken up and hard to drive on. I meet a couple of graders but no trucks and just a couple of pickups. Go over several streams – they seem hardly frozen – at least it seems the ice is clear.

By mid-afternoon I pull into Coldfoot. It seems a nice spot for a camp. I meet another Alyeska auditor, Bob Thomas, get my room assignment and go there. I find the one bed not made. Conclusion:No rooms are as nice as Happy or Galbraith. There are trees here around the buildings and I saw a squirrel.

I try to figure out a place for camera and equipment but finally give up and use some time cleaning up. Dick arrived about 4:00 p.m. He seems more mellow for some reason. Maybe it did him good to do the driving by himself rather than sleeping in the car. After dinner I read the Rasputin book for awhile and turned in early.

NOW IT'S DECEMBER 25 and a lonely Christmas at Coldfoot. I tried to call Bob last night, but he either wasn't home or just not answering. I do miss him. I have learned how much it means to have someone – on the holidays and all. It would be unbearable without Bob. Well, they did put on quite a good holiday dinner:

turkey, dressing with raisins and nuts, and pumpkin pie with ice cream for dessert. Then I spent a long evening reading Rasputin.

We spend the next day just buzzing around Coldfoot. It's not cold but breezy and bitter. We spend a portion of the day after 10:00 a.m. (when Steve comes in by plane from spending Christmas at home) taking photos. There's no real rush and by 2:00 p.m. we are all finished until the night shift starts at 5:00. We meet the NANA crew with Drake Rowe as sergeant. He takes me around in his pickup for photos. I got a nice shot of an old cabin with tracks leading out. Coldfoot proved to be a nice, clean camp with two rec rooms, a sauna, and a good library.

In the morning we leave about 9:00 a.m. and head for Dietrich. The scenery along the way is gorgeous as the road winds through a long, broad valley. The mountains are beautiful, but the road has no steep grades. I drive, naturally, while Dick sleeps. We arrive well before noon and set up in a conference room in the Arctic offices. For the next two hours we are very busy, but by 1:00 p.m. we are almost done. I go to lunch and meet my old roommate, Jean Layman. We wind up work just before dinner. Later I met Jean and Lt. Earl Hibspman and also saw Red Jaynes, who was a driver for Gilman's Bakery in Anchorage at the time I worked there. I spent the evening shooting the breeze with them.

Our drive the next morning on the way to Chandalar was through some really great scenery. Tall and impressive mountains. Too bad it was too dark to see everything, but I was able to get a good idea of what it's like.

It was only 35 miles to the camp, which is very small and sits on a hillside. We do all the badges there real fast. The camp population is small and partly shutdown with only porta-potties in use.

We are on the way to Atigun before lunch. It was a disappointment. The day was real cloudy and we can't see much, but I do dimly see tall, snowy peaks. We take photos all afternoon and I hear a rumor that Happy is closing. A real blow if true.

For some reason or other, Atigun repels me. Probably from my past experience at road checks at Galbraith when I found Atigun residents cliquish. It was a nice-looking, freshly-painted camp, though.

On to Galbraith by 8:30 a.m. and set up in the recently enlarged messhall. I see many old friends, and Kay the bullcook is still there. She helps me find an unused room in P Barracks. The dinner is delicious – baked chicken. The best since I have been on the line. I hear again that Happy is closing but I call Mishko and he says no, it's just a rumor.

WE SET OFF THE NEXT MORNING at 8:30 for Toolik. We had only 11 miles to go. Dick had wanted to have his Suburban fixed,but the auditor says no because he is leaving by plane for the 31st and the 1st. We forge on with Dick put out by the hurry. We set up in the messhall and are rushed by work. The whole camp files by without a stop. By noon we're almost finished, and I take some time to look around outside. Toolik is a nice camp, small but nicely finished. The food is good with lots of salads and good desserts and a steak for dinner.

124

Chapter 13

The next day I am over to the messhall just after 6:00 a.m. Two or three people dribble in for photos, but the day is spent doing almost nothing. Dick finally folds up the equipment and we quit work. The day is not nice – snowy and warm – but we will stay here until tomorrow, which will be next year! The people here are nice, they want us to go to the New Year's Eve party. I think about it but decide to stay in my room and read a Gothic novel until late. Some New Year's.

The next morning I am awakened by my roommate about 5:30. I get up, shower, wash my hair, get ready, have breakfast and make an early start for Happy Valley. Dick is going in the auditor's Suburban. I had a good trip by myself. The scenery was nice even though it is dark out. I came upon long stretches of the pipe in place. The country is rolling with long grades and some quite steep. However, these spots were sanded and were no problem. Driving into Happy I saw two foxes – mistook them at first for wolverines. There were ravens on the ground and foxes apparently looking for food dropped by the ravens. I had seen this before. Apparently they are companions, one feeding the other.

I go first to find the bullcook and get a room but have no luck. There's no one in the office, but Mishko finally wanders in. He said he thought we would be in to spend New Year's. He has a nice single room for me: N-17. I wish now I had come on home to Happy yesterday.

Spent the midday driving around for both color and black and white of the surroundings. I had dinner with the lieutenant and Mishko. (The only decorations were empty booze bottles.) The cook said the new rule is steak now once every 10 days instead of once a week. Mishko came in to chat after dinner. He stayed to talk about his property – he now owns a four-plex, a house, and five lots in Anchorage. A smart guy, he may well end up a millionaire.

The next day I had little time to do anything but work. We set up the badging operation in the messhall and spent all day there from about 8:00 a.m. until 7:00 p.m. and got all 130 Happy Valley residents. That's amazing to me that the residents of that big and bustling camp have dwindled down to really just a handful. But that's the story all along the line with the winter shut-down.

On the 3rd, we once again get up early, eat break-fast, and load gear. We depart for Franklin Bluffs by 7:00 a.m. but it's a mixed-up trip. Steve, the auditor, does not go because his car broke down just about five miles out. Then we have to turn around and go back to Happy to re-trieve the backdrop from the messhall. We finally get underway and it is all dark along the way. I do manage to pick out some features of the land and can see lights a long way off. We drop down from the heights and never seem to actually climb again. We drop in at deserted PS-2, which Dick used to guard, but there's not much to see.

About 10:30 we arrive at Franklin. We finish quickly – there's only about 25 residents – and have lunch here. I spent some time shooting Franklin, which is a simply stunning location. A range of intriguing, far-away mountains is the horizon to the east and north. I get many good shots of the bluffs, buildings, ravens, machin-ery, and of the nice operator, John Duff.

But the really fascinating view is of those distant mountains which create perfect examples of "ice city mirage." I have to explain here just what that is. Bob and I first saw this when we lived in our home on Government Hill in Anchorage. The big window in our dining room gave a perfect view down Turnagain Arm and Cook Inlet. When conditions were just right – particularly on cold winter days – you could look down the inlet and the distant, snowy mountains across the water were distorted into shapes that looked just like tall skyscraper buildings. If you didn't know better, you would swear you were looking at a distant shining city. It was the same effect here at Franklin.

NOW IT'S ON NORTH TO PRUDHOE and the northern end of the line. The starting point for the whole production and pipeline operation. The view on the way north was spectacular in its own way. At times we could see almost 360 degrees to the horizon. The road was straight and good and there was not much traffic. Our vehicle was not in the best of shape – the speedometer is gone and the heater is no good. But it limps along okay.

We follow the bluffs for a long distance. Quite interesting. The rest of the landscape resembles the ocean, with the snow as waves. There's a glow to the east and south, but to the north and west it is quite dark. The horizon there is indistinct. Dick is sleepy as I continue driving. We pass through one gate on the main road and start seeing many lights. It's as if the landscape is dotted with many camps, which it is. Prudhoe is now the fourth largest settlement in Alaska, with 7,000 to 8,000 people.

The wind picks up. Prudhoe is known for strong winds, and it lives up to its billing. We find the first gate manned by Jeff Maurer – he deserves this! A good place for him. At the gate we run into Lieutenant Tomlinson, who has been in Franklin. We drive on following him. I can see now why people ask about the road from here on. There is constant wind and drifting snow – real ground blizzards – making the road hard to follow.

At the second guard gate we meet Harry Prator – I'm so glad to see him again and him me. We also meet a new Eskimo guard, Roy Mendenhall. This is a desolate spot. Lights of the camps are dim now because of snow in the air. We continue behind the Lieutenant – what a mess – with roads shooting off in every direction. The lieutenant does miss the way once and then we meet a car which is ahead of a wide load. After turning around in the road several times following the lieutenant, we continue on and edge past a truck loaded with a huge crane. The tracks of the machine are really wide. Shortly we come into the PS-1 settlement. We stop at another gate shack, which, it turns out, is NANA's only office here. We go on into camp and stop at the Innkeeper's where a woman assigns me Room C114. Dick will stay with the lieutenant. We unload things and I find the place very clean, in fact immaculate.

Later I accompany Dick to the Fluor-Alyeska offices and make arrangements for setting up the ID operation. We meet the Big Boss, Chuck Bennett, who is short, oldish, crusty, and has not much use for NANA. He never does say a word to me, except hello. Churlish. Oafish. He will not hear of us setting up in the messhall.

He meets this suggestion with an outraged roar. Oh, well. We went to supper at 7:15.

I meet Karen Arsenault and Annette, both guards, then go on to my room for a long nice, but cold evening reading *Jamaica Inn*.

We're up early the next day and to work by 9:00 a.m., but Dick says we are not to do many because today is Sunday and it's a double-time day. They do not want workers badged on a double-time day. We finish by 11:00 and take off in the car to see the sights. It's a nice clear, cold day and we cover the entire area. We stop at the NANA Hotel and find lunch here $15 each, so no lunch. We later talked to the manager who said, as NANA people, we could have had lunch free. Phooey!

By the time we are outside, about 1:00 p.m., the sun is already setting. Daylight here is only about an hour or a little more. The sunglow around the horizon lasts until 5:00 p.m. We see many lights around the area, lighted oil rigs and flares, dozens of settlements and roads.

We visit the Arco building and then drive out to watch work on the causeway and barges. It's a very spectacular operation with giant earth-movers bringing fill. We park right on top of what is likely the Arctic Ocean,with huge cakes of ice on either side of the road. There's much activity, as a big crane operates a metal net, which dredges up ice, then is swiftly followed by dumped fill.

THE NEXT DAY WE START on our return trip south. I'm up at 5:00 a.m. after reading until midnight.

The entire morning is spent badging with a steady stream of people. Then we pack up and leave, stopping first at the BP building, which is indeed fancy with a swimming pool, and an enclosed solarium where people play tennis, jog and so forth. There are trees in glass cases and beautiful lounges. Then we drive out of town and decide to spend the night at Franklin. We find it is not the best, as facilities are closed down and you can only urinate in two barracks. For more serious business you have to use porta-potties.

We stop at Happy Valley early in the morning. Dick wants to stay for lunch, but since he has the auditor's vehicle and I have one I decide to go on. I was glad I did because I got some nice photos. I saw caribou in a long string out on the snowy tundra and always the pipe. I arrived at Pump Station 3 and admired its location, better than I thought. It has a backdrop of nice peaks and much interesting nearby scenery. I set up in the conference room and try to tell the manager that I don't want a bunch of people at once – only a few at a time – but this is difficult to get across. Almost at once, people start arriving and soon I'm working full speed. Dick arrives about 3:00 p.m. and we take 88 pictures by 6:00 p.m. We quit for the day and after dinner I spend the evening reading. PS-3 turns out to be very friendly and nice.

Just a small breakfast the next day. I decide I must start eating less. I feel so full and awful, and I have gained weight. There's been a lack of exercise on this expedition – not like walking guard duty. We work until 10:30 and then fold up. The day is beautiful and I go around taking a few pictures. I leave for Toolik before noon so I can get pix there. But light is already lousy when I arrive, so I just have coffee and then go on to Galbraith. The long hills seem rounded and the light is beautiful around the horizon. I get pictures of dark peaks and light on frozen lakes.

In Galbraith I get rooms and talk to people and I find many who have come back from R & R without new badges. Dick arrives about 4:00 p.m. and I tell him about this. We try to spread the word around that we'll set up in PS-4 tomorrow.

Next morning I get to Pump 4 ahead of Dick and get the whole thing set up in the rec hall with the aid of the RCM. I ask him to send people through slowly and he agrees. I work some time before Dick arrives and am doing okay. After he arrives we work almost straight through. After a poor night's sleep, I go and load up the equipment. I ask one man to help me carry gear but he grumbles about "scabbing" so I more or less tell him to go to hell and do it myself. This is a crappy camp. A woman worker tells me there are only 10 women here and the RCM wishes there were none. The rest room is so tiny it will hardly accommodate two at a time.

I'm glad to get on the road again, but Dick finally shows up and says the Suburban has a flat. He has to go back to Galbraith to get the tire fixed and I decide to follow him. We agree we must stick together because of the possibility of car trouble. We have no emergency gear, not even a radio or sleeping bag.

We spend until after lunch at Galbraith getting the car in shape. The weather is not good. It was snowing earlier and is overcast as we start out. Stop for pix on the road between Galbraith and PS-4. I see a wolf above Atigun. He is trotting along beside the road. He circles the vehicle and is very wary.

It is very much an experience going over the pass, especially down the south side. It is very stormy and the pass is *steep*. On the south side there is a beautiful sunset and we can see a long, long way. Big trucks transporting ATCO units are on their way up, one being pulled by a road grader. I inch down and make it fine – a long, long grade. It's well sanded, so no problem. Think about it unsanded – wow!

Stop at the bottom of the grade for pix of the last spruce tree going north. From here on we will have trees again. We make another stop at Dietrich for coffee and go to the NANA office where we meet Sergeant Reynolds and shoot the breeze for a long time. Finally head out and drive on to Coldfoot where it is *cold* – 55 below! We stay there for the night. I have a solo room in the men's barracks, but must go over to the women's to use facilities. Silly.

NO WARM AIR FROM my heater as we head on south in the morning. I keep close to Dick's car, which means I'm driving in his fog. My feet feel frozen, my hands too. I'm wearing waffle stompers and my feet are so cold I'm really worried.

Dick finally stops and comes back and I give him my shoe pacs to get warmed up in his car. After a time we stop again and I change into them – feet warm up fast. We pull into Prospect and secure rooms, then go on to PS-5. See Jean at the gate and ask her about getting my car fixed – I figure she knows everyone. However, I meet the head mechanic at lunch and make arrangements to get the heater fixed.

We set up in the rec hall and work through the day. Work here is our lowest point. I find it hard to take Fluor pix and make many errors. No typist is available and I have to take over that job. This leaves Dick working alone. He is a very disorganized person, and gets badges mixed up, I'm almost positive. However, I couldn't care less and simply do not worry. We finish about 3:30, put everything in the cars but have to wait for gas. So it's close to 9:00 when I finally get to relax and read the rest of my novel.

As we head south the next morning, my Blazer is acting up again – this time the brake light. We drive slowly and carefully and stop at Old Man, as Dick has a nail in his tire and I have to get more antifreeze. We end up staying for lunch and then drive on until about 3:00 p.m. to Five Mile Camp. Lots of truck traffic. This 30-mile stretch hasn't been sanded. Going down one hill, I step on the brake as a big truck comes roaring up. The car slides, I hastily remove my foot from the brake and throw the gear shift into low. Very frightening for a minute.

The scenery along here is stunning. The trees are heavily frosted and the sky is pink. We have caught up with the sun, which is almost but not quite visible through the sunset clouds. We stop several times along the way to look for tracks and to take pix.

I am surprised to find that Five Mile is a very likable small camp. Only 102 people. The RCM is very nice and we have no trouble securing single rooms. The units are different – somewhat like the old 20-man units at Happy. It's very hot in my room but fortunately the window will open. The food turns out to be delicious. This is IT. I had always pictured Five Mile as not very desirable, but I was wrong. The people are really great – including the NANA people. These include Sgt. Russ Campbell a very nice older man.

Next day I find the Blazer in bad condition. Also Steve's Suburban will not start. The head-bolt heater isn't working. We decide the Blazer must be worked on before proceeding. We take a NANA Suburban while the Blazer is in the shop. We start badging about 10:00 a.m. and work all day. People are well scheduled, and there is no rush. We work until 8:00 p.m., so I have no time to read as we must leave early for PS-6.

WE HEAD FOR ONE OF OUR last stops in the morning. We just have PS-6 and Livengood Camp left on this expedition. Stop for coffee at Five Mile and then go on to PS-6. We find that this one of nicest of the pump stations. The food is very good. This is Grey-hound. We catch the last of our workers and we're back at Five Mile by mid-morning. I check on the Blazer and find it's OK. Having been in the shop all night it has thawed and now runs fine.

After lunch we take off for Livengood and Fair-banks. It's only 56 miles to Livengood, but we stop often. There is a full moon and the scenery is grand. The trees are all heavy with snow and frost. The Valley of Yukon is beautiful. We stop atop the last hill for pix and also before the bridge for pix of the pipe and moon. Dick decides not to wait. I am enjoying the scenery, so I do not go very fast. After Dick is gone, I remember that I don't know where Livengood camp is located. And it's fast getting dark. Wonder how I'll find it.

Pass the junction of Manley and Yukon River Road and I drive some miles toward the village. It's very dark now. At the bottom of a hill I see a loaded truck coming and get it to stop by blinking the lights. The young driver says the camp is off about a mile on Manley Road. He is not upset because of the stop. I turn around, go back and on to camp. I find that Dick arrived just 20 minutes ago.

I get a room in a new kind of 56-man unit. The hallway is shiny and clean, the room nice, but warm. The bath and rest rooms are used by men *and* women! I'm not too keen on this arrangement. I take a shower and find the stalls have big cracks along the sides. I hope to heaven Dick doesn't decide to shower in the next stall.

This is a Boatel concession and the food is not so good. The camp is okay – better than I had imagined – but confirms my idea that I would not like working in the southern camps. There are only about 10 women in a camp of 102.

We spend all day taking badge photos. I didn't scout around outside because I'm not especially interested in this camp. Just before we fold up this last of our camps, Dick suggests we make a bunch of ID badges for ourselves. We spend a relaxing and jovial time trying to think of every single different situation where we might need ID.

The Blazer is again in bad shape the next morning as we leave for Fairbanks. It is barely pooping along, going up hills at about 5 miles an hour. We stop at Livengood, hoping to get coffee at Sam's, but he is not open. I drive the Blazer at high speed back to the junction, trying to get the carbon out. It seems to help a lot.

We stop several times en route. Dick looks for tracks. We explore a small trail and take pictures. The scenery is nice but becomes less spectacular the further south we go. Lots and lots of trucks heading north. We are glad we aren't up there on Atigun Pass.

Make a stop at Fox for hamburgers and coffee. Then on into Fairbanks about 1:00 p.m. We check into our respective hotels – Traveler's Inn for me – then go to the NANA offices for our paychecks. We meet both Bill Nix and Jim Miller. Nix quite friendly and I mention the possibility of a book later about NANA. He seems receptive, and shows me files.

It's not really cold in Fairbanks, only about minus 12. Later I meet Dick and have a beer at the Golden Nugget Lodge. He is plastered. I leave and have a sandwich at Traveler's. I'm feeling very tired and get to bed by 9:30.

And thus ends the Great Re-Badging Expedition.

The Men and Their Unions

Once we completed the Great Re-Badging Expedition, I returned home to Happy Valley and my regular duties as a security guard, making the rounds and checking barracks and furnaces. It was a very quiet camp now – many barracks were empty – and there was only a skeleton, winter crew of residents. It was a mighty cold camp, too. This was February and the temperatures were staying well below zero. There was one incident at this time that broke up the routine and boredom. I was approached by someone from the union who asked if I would be interested in becoming a union steward. I told him I would have to think long and hard about it.

Every time I hear someone saying something about "the union" or think about what a big role the craft unions were playing in this giant construction job, my mind goes back to those two old-time workers I described earlier. Those were the two old men who thought women should be totally barred from the union and the jobs. They were men who had spent all of their working days in what amounted to an all-boys club.

Of course, their views weren't original or theirs alone. Probably just about all of the older men workers felt somewhat the same way, along with a share of the younger men. But, fortunately for me and all the other women on the job, the times were changing and, hopefully things would never go back to what they were before this pipeline job.

This giant construction job has been compared in size and scope to other projects such as the digging of the Panama Canal through the jungles of Central America, and the building of the Alaska Highway through the Canadian wilderness during World War II. From what all I have been able to read, only a handful of women were able to take part in those jobs. They only played minor roles in filling the "traditional" jobs offered women – such as nurses, teachers, and office workers.

Thankfully, that's not true of this massive project. Making the rounds on my job at Galbraith and Happy Valley, and visiting all of the northern camps and pump stations while re-badging, I compiled a list of all of the different jobs where I found women working. Now, admittedly, in some cases, there were only one or two women filling these "masculine" spots – but it is a start, and hopefully things will go forward from here rather than slipping back again to all-boys clubs. My list of jobs women are filling here and now: a welder, mechanics, electricians, security guards, radio operators, culinary workers, pilots, recreation directors, laborers, truck drivers and medics.

There was always the old claim that women couldn't do such jobs – and particularly on a remote wilderness project – because "women always cause trouble" on the job. But it's been my experience that when there is trouble between men and women at work, in nine cases out of ten, it's the man who causes the trouble and that's to be expected. In nine cases out of ten, men are more aggressive than women. For instance, it's hard to imagine a group of women forming a mob or trying to cause a riot. But it's not difficult to imagine a group of men doing that. We had just such a case at Galbraith while I was working there.

I already described how the electricians at Galbraith caused all sorts of trouble in the first months I worked there. They caused dozens and dozens of false fire alarms for no other reason but that in each case, an electrician on standby had to be called in to re-set the alarm at overtime pay rates. As I mentioned, the situation finally got so bad that the whole lot of these workers were discharged and ordered off the line.

What I didn't go on to tell about, is what happened next. There was a loud, rowdy all-night drinking party in Barracks R, which housed a majority of the electrical workers. This was followed by what amounted to a near-riot at the Galbraith airport.

That R Barracks already had a reputation as the "partying" barracks but there had been nothing to compare with the night before the electricians were shipped out. R always reeked with the sweet smell of pot. There were always more fire alarms and loud parties there than any other barracks. It was a strange thing about these electrical workers. I had never known before that an entire trade could be so clannish and troublesome. Also, they seemed to be particularly disliked by the other crafts. The night mechanics were downright glad they had been fired. The foreman of the mechanics told me this, and said the electrical workers were snobbish, holding themselves "better" than mechanics, carpenters, and plumbers.

Whatever the facts, that last night before they left became a little bit of hell for the security guards. I came on the first party in R early in my beat. The hallway was crowded and people were standing around loaded, with drinks in hand.

I was very mild and only asked one of the group if he would tell the others to keep the noise down. The last round, before it broke up, it looked as though a fist fight might be brewing. Again, I appealed for help and finally all became quiet. I went into the furnace room and when I came out the entire group had disappeared, leaving paper cups sitting in the firehose box. But as time went on that night, the parties became more violent. On Eric's shift he said he had to lay down the law, which did actually get results. That was pretty much the end of the night's activity.

But the next day – the actual shipping out day – was the payoff. It took the entire day shift including the lieutenant, the sergeant, Dennis and Ray Leach all day at the airport trying to keep the outgoing electricians in line. Much of the trouble came from the continued drunkenness and from the fact that the men tried to beat their way onto planes too small to contain them. For instance, when the first plane came in, it had 28 seats but there were 125 drunken would-be passengers trying to get aboard. Ray Leach said he had never seen a more obstreperous bunch even in his many years in the military.

The camp was quiet the night of the shipping out. I patrolled B Area, which includes all of the 52 and 56-man barracks. The lieutenant said he had a few parties getting started, so I approached my shift with wary feelings. There was the usual pot smell and a few doors were open but no activity like the night before. At one open door which I passed with haste and no looks to right or left, a loud voice always called out: "Hello, Wilma". I always said, "Hello to you too," though I had no idea who it was.

Actually I have had very little trouble with the men here when they were either drunk or sober. Except for the occasional character who seems to be mad at the entire world, I seem to be able to get along with just about everyone. The fact that I am older – and wearing a uniform – probably helps a lot. As I have mentioned earlier, I try to be friendly with all the people I meet and maintain a personal-impersonal attitude.

I've tried to never show a long face or act in a surly manner. I think most of the people – men and women – appreciate a show of friendliness and cheerfulness. While some of the men put on a show of hoping for something more, I am of the opinion it is a relief to find they can just be friendly and natural. I believe just having women as part of the scene at these camps is a good thing.

Personally, I have been treated with utmost courtesy, almost without exception. And even with loving kindness that is often very touching if not almost embarrassing. One man, whose name I do not even know, was always particularly nice. Just before he left on R & R, he and a truck driver known as Yogi were sitting in the theater when I went through. He stopped me and said he was going out for two weeks and I wished him the best of all good times. He took my hand and patted it and said:

"You know, I want you to understand how much I have appreciated having such a nice person as you around!"

I was really floored. Certainly it was a wonderful compliment and it made any efforts of mine worthwhile.

On the other hand, younger women on the job – and most of the women here are quite young – often have to put up with a lot more problems with some of the men. There is harassment from time to time and every time I see a woman having a problem, I feel it is part of my duty to step in and cool things off. Women also have problems at times with job discrimination. Take the case of Rosie, a homely little laborer from Fairbanks. She works at the sewage treatment plant and she really had some problems there. The way I heard it, she had seniority with the Laborers at this camp. When the day incinerator job needed filling, Rosie applied for the job, and got it. Then the old guy who also worked at the plant quit and said he wasn't going to work for a "damned woman."

Rosie proved she could do the job and yet they were going to fire her and give the job to the old guy. So she just filed a suit through the Laborers' Union and the state employment people. From what I hear, the state really jumped in there fast and got her put back on the job and the old guy kicked out. And Arctic Constructors had to back down. The thing is almost over with Rosie way up there on top, so things are looking up. I want to go down and get a picture of Rosie.

It's something else again to be working in a world that has traditionally been men's since the year one (no women working on the Great Pyramids, I'll bet!), and is still considered to be so by the majority of people here. I chalk this one up in the "For" column in the mental scorecard I'm keeping as I think about the Union.

One thing I mention to women who ask about getting jobs in this almost wholly male environment, is that you have to get over any feeling of embarrassment in personal situations. As an example, I tell how about in making my rounds I often come across male workers in less than complete clothing. Just the other night while checking the furnaces and water heaters in the 20-man units, I went through the open bathroom area between sleeping units. There I came across the head man here with Arctic Constructors, Bob Norman. He was standing around by the sinks talking to other top brass. He said:

"Hello, Wilma. How are you?" I said: "Hello, Bob. Nice to see you. Haven't seen you around, have you been on R & R?" He said yes. All this very nonchalant with him standing there in his shorts. Neither of us was embarrassed or cracked a smile – just chatted like old friends meeting on the street.

I used to be embarrassed if I came upon fellows in their shorts – and a few in less – or standing in the little alcoves at the urinals, but no more. And I think they aren't concerned, either. Naturally, if they're standing at the urinals, I refrain from clapping them on the back and saying "Hi!" but I don't back out either, just continue on my rounds. The only concession I make is to refrain from trying to identify them, and just go on my way.

If a woman is going to work in this almost exclusively-male environment the only way she can do it successfully is with a certain attitude. I've thought so much about this problem for a female security guard, that I came up with this 12-point guide:

1. She will have to overcome physical cow-ardliness.

2. She must accept the day-to-day grind that men have had to learn to accept.

3. She must act in such a manner as to pre-serve dignity and integrity.

4. She must not expect concessions because she is a female. (If she isn't healthy she should not compete.)

5. Don't flaunt femaleness and sex, or be coy.

6. Don't try to act like a man, or become tough, obscene, or loud-mouthed.

7. Develop a bit of humility. Try not to be moody, or perverse.

8. Do more than expected.

10. Abide by company and job rules

11. Don't belittle men (I remember a truck driver who helped a woman change a tire and said: "I didn't know it was ever out of style to help a fellow human").

12. Don't try to punish men because they've had it so good for so long and women have had it so bad.

I don't know if my rules will solve every problem, for every woman, in every situation, but they have sure been helpful for me.

My Not-So-Restful R&R

No matter where you go on the pipeline, anytime you come across a couple of the workers shooting the breeze, there is one phrase you are mostly likely to hear them mention: R & R. That's the magic symbol and the biggest topic of conversation for every pipeline worker. It stands for "Rest and Relaxation," that wonderful vacation, that period of your time off from the job. It's what everyone looks forward to week after week while working. Its starting date is the day that you circle on your calendar and you continue to X off the days, one by one, until it arrives.

The vacation schedule can vary somewhat from job to job, but here at NANA Security, it calls for eight weeks of work followed by two weeks off. I think that is probably about average for most pipeline workers. While most of us are counting the days until the start of our next R & R, there are a few people who go for much longer work periods with no time off. They are mostly workers who have some immediate goal in mind for their pipeline dollars, and the extra money they earn by staying on the job is more important to them than any rest and relaxation time.

One of these unusual people was Bud, the little old bullcook I mentioned earlier, who liked to lean on his mop handle while chatting and spitting tobacco juice in the mop bucket. For many years he had made a career of working wilderness jobs and saving money to buy up farmland back in his home state. He told me that once, working at Barter Island, he had gone 26 months with no break.

I wasn't one of the unusual people, and by the time I had my first five weeks in, I was checking the calendar and counting off the days until I could leave on my R & R. I worked out my schedule and wrote Bob with the days for my three scheduled vacations that first year: June 2, 1975, August 18, and November 3. Oddly enough, as things worked out, I was able to do Bud a favor he requested while I was on my first vacation and Bud was back in camp leaning on his mop and racking up the dollars.

The first month on the job really went by pretty fast, but then the reality set in when I realized I still had four more weeks to go. One night in the office, Eric and I had a long discussion about The Job versus prison and there did seem to be a lot of similarities.

For a few days just before that, I had been feeling really let down and kept asking myself if I could stand it (though I realized I almost had to). This had seriously affected my relationship with everybody, which was too bad but I suppose it was bound to happen. As Eric explained it, this was my 5-week letdown. That day I was in terrible shape and just wanted to sit down and cry. The whole idea of the job was insupportable. I think this happens to everyone – some actually leave on account of it, or go out and get drunk.

Fortunately, the next day was gorgeous and, determined to get over my gloom, I took my camera and went out and got some color shots. I got some of the girl

Laborers and other people down around the Helipad. While talking to the pilot, he said he had to make a short trip around the area and asked if I would like to go along. Of course! That helicopter ride gave a chance to see our whole area from the air and really capped off a beautiful day.

I made a vow right then to try for a more positive outlook and to spend my time thinking about all the things I would get done during my R & R.

To help pass the time, I made up a little list of things to do during the vacation. The "do at home" list included: Making two trousers and one jacket; shop; bake turkeys and bread; shorten the length and sleeves of the gray shirts. This list was in addition to the errand I had to attend to for Bullcook Bud. It involved his late uncle Eddie Holland, who according to Bud, was in the 1898 gold rush and wound up years later working a gold claim he staked up in the Talkeetna Mountains.

Anyway, Eddie Holland built a cabin on his claim, where he lived. One day, while he was working outside, the cabin caught fire. Apparently, Eddie rushed in to save something – gold, guns, a dog?– and he was badly burned. So much so that he died after dragging himself nine miles to a neighbor's for help. Bud said Eddie was buried in a cemetery located, as he put it, on the edge of Anchorage. Without a doubt this was the old Anchorage City Cemetery at Sixth and Cordova, which the city has now grown up around.

Bud said one of the biggest things in his life would be to get a photo of Eddie's grave, if a marker exists.

Chapter 15

Well, to tell the whole story, during my first R & R, I visited that cemetery, which is not in the best of shape these days. But with the help of the caretaker I was able to locate Eddie's grave. It had just a ground-level marker but no headstone. When I got back to camp I was able to report this to Bud, and he vowed to set some money aside and get a proper headstone installed.

As it turned out, I had plenty of time during that first "vacation" to run the errand for Bud, as well as to alter my uniforms and shirts, do my necessary shopping, and to cook those two turkeys. (I can no longer remember *why* I wanted to cook two turkeys). Yes, I had plenty of time to do all that because Bob was just too busy with his magazine job to spend much time with me. He seemed to have become very distant, and, in all, it was a very disappointing vacation. It was almost a pleasure when it ended and I could go back to camp. Galbraith seemed more my home now than my Anchorage home.

My second R & R, which came along in mid-August started out much better and on a cheerful note. We had long planned a trip "outside" flying to Seattle and then renting a car and driving across the state to visit my half-sister Alma (mother of Millie) in her home in Haines, Oregon. Rather surprisingly, Bob was still in favor of making the trip. Just a day after I arrived home in Anchorage, we boarded an Alaska Airlines plane and flew to Seattle where we spent the night and picked up our rental car early the next morning.

That car proved to be a real surprise to us in many ways. For some reason – just luck of the draw, I guess – the rental agency assigned us a brand new Pontiac Sunbird. It was a striking vehicle to say the least: A sporty-looking hard top two-door coupe with just seven miles on the odometer. To top things off, it was polished and shiny, and bright yellow in color!

That car drew a lot of attention as we started our trip. We noticed that in a couple of towns we passed through, some people walking along would actually stop and stare at the vehicle. Apparently it was a brand new model and the first car of its type seen in this area. But the car also got some attention that wasn't so positive. We stopped in one of the towns for lunch and when we came out of the cafe, Bob noticed a small puddle of oil on the pavement under the rear axle. This was a real problem: It meant the differential was leaking.

That meant we had to stop our trip right there and locate an Pontiac dealer. We did find the dealer, took it into the shop, and the leak was stopped. A couple of hours later we were on the road again. We were okay for now, but trouble like that in such a new vehicle seemed to bode ill and gave us both sort of an uneasy feeling.

Nevertheless, we continued on our way and spent the next couple of days on a leisurely trip across Washington and Oregon. We enjoyed the scenery, visited some of the tourist spots, and had a pretty fun time of it. It was almost like old times traveling together, leaving our routines behind and forgetting our troubles and worries. (There was one jarring note: Bob took the time to make a couple of collect phone calls to his office to make sure things were going the way he wanted.)

The next bump in our road came as we were approaching Baker City, the nearest town of any size (population about 9,000) to Alma's location. The car felt rather stuffy, and Bob went to roll his side window down. It went down, all right.

With a loud *Clunk!* the whole window dropped to the bottom inside the door. It refused to come back up. That made driving rather uncomfortable, and if it should start to rain we really would be in trouble.

We headed north from Baker City and drove about a dozen miles to reach Haines, which was a tiny community of a few hundred, located off the Interstate on the old U.S. 30 route. We finally managed to locate Alma. She had a job house sitting an old rambling ranch house for absentee owners who were off on an extended trip. I always enjoyed visiting Alma, and the next couple of days were no exception. Alma was a large, motherly woman a number of years older than me. She always seemed friendly and happy to have visitors. Sadly, although I didn't know it at the time, this was the last chance I had to visit her before her death.

Haines, being a really small community, there was just one garage in town, and it didn't look too promising. However, Alma said the mechanic at the garage had a good reputation, so we left the Sunbird with him in hopes he could get something done to that window before we had to make the trip back across the state and up to Seattle. As it turned out he was unable to get the necessary parts to repair the window, but he did manage to get it completely closed and then wired it up so it would stay shut.

THE HAPPY DAYS WE were able to spend with Alma went by rapidly. Way too fast. Alma always put on a happy face for visitors and seemed pretty content with her lot in life. That, despite the fact that she didn't have a really easy time of it having to take jobs as a ranch cook or house-sitting as she was doing now. But she didn't let any troubles show. And even Bob seemed in a good mood and spent a lot of time with her chatting about life in her small town and on the various ranches in the area.

For my part, I just enjoyed being in a completely different place with a climate and landscape totally unlike the Arctic. I took several long walks around various parts of the ranch just savoring the views and watching the livestock. About the only thing I really missed was a horse to ride!

Then, all too soon, we had to pack up our things, say our goodbyes to Alma, and head back north. We were leaving the happy days behind and returning to where all our cares and worries still awaited us. It was with a real feeling of dread that I climbed into the Sunbird, waved goodbye to Alma, and we started on the trip to Seattle. The trip back was an anti-climax. In contrast to our leisurely trip over, we drove almost straight through. We had very little to say to each other – I suppose we were both thinking about the troubled times that faced us back in Alaska. That trip back in the Sunbird and then the flight to Anchorage was pretty grim, and it seemed our few happy days in Haines were already fading into the distant past.

Chapter 15

I would learn in the months to come that this bittersweet trip to Oregon would be the last time Bob and I traveled together while I was in the Arctic. By the time my next R & R rolled around we were hardly on speaking terms.

From there, things went right on down hill. When I would go to Anchorage on R & R, we would always end up in a bitter argument. When I was in camp, it seemed that my letter writing and picture taking all fell by the wayside. I felt miserable as I tried to look ahead and figure out what was going to happen once my job was over and it all just seemed a blank. While I realized that Bob no longer seemed to care about any plans for us for the future, I felt that I had to have some general idea of what was to come for me.

I thought about our problems at length as I went on my rounds. Sometimes they seemed really dreadful – especially what faced me – how I'd sort of fallen apart. Mentally and physically I seemed to be just a real loss to Bob and myself. I can't even tell what a nightmare it is to wake up one morning and face such a thing.

I tried not to think about it. But, too, I realized other people must go through the same things – after all, no one stays young. And I have seen many people, older and alone, who appear to be happy for one reason or another. Maybe there is still some hope for me.

The Oil Starts to Flow

June 20, 1977. That was the magic date. That was the day the Alyeska officials at Pump Station No. 1 at Prudhoe turned the tap, pushed the button, or did whatever they had to do to start the first oil flowing down the newly-completed pipeline on its five-day-long trip to Valdez. It was a magical day all right, but it hardly came as a surprise. Those of us working as NANA Security guards had been expecting this event for weeks and even months. And we looked forward to the day with something like a feeling of dread.

The start of production meant the end of the construction days and the closing of what had become a way of life during the years we had been working in the Arctic. It meant the closing of a chapter in our lives and the closing down of the camps like Happy Valley, which had come to seem like home.

In my more than 26 months on the job, I had witnessed almost the complete cycle of construction. Work on the project started in March, 1975 and by the next month I was working at the Galbraith camp. On May 23rd of 1977, I personally closed down one of the camps – Toolik – by pulling a chain across the entrance gate and securing it with a padlock.

I'd always had sort of a soft spot for Toolik Camp, and it was sad to have to close it down. Toolik was a small camp and I had never spent much time working there, but I had visited a time or two. While the camp

154

was small, it was nicely laid out and finished and the people there seemed friendly and on the happy side. Now it would stand idle and empty until the wreckers came along and either tore down its buildings or moved them away. Soon it would be nothing but an empty spot in the Arctic wilderness.

The closing of Toolik came along quite awhile after the first signs that construction was winding down and my job was coming to an end. People I had known for many months in camp had started to disappear. They weren't headed outside on R & R – their jobs had ended and they had been terminated. When I went out to the airport I noted that outgoing flights left fully loaded, while the incoming planes carried only a minimum of passengers.

Meanwhile, things were also changing for us guards at NANA Security. There appeared to be a lot of thrashing around amongst the higher-ups. It appeared from all the signs that NANA Security would also be shutting down as construction came to an end. Some of the same officials who had headed our company were busy organizing a new non-union outfit, Purcell Security.

Many of the NANA guards were in the process of switching over to this new outfit even before construction ended. Personally, I wasn't interested. Working with the new security company didn't appeal to me, and, frankly, I just wanted to get away for awhile.

After 26 months on the job in the Arctic I was just plain tired – mentally and physically. My health wasn't the best, and my personal life was in a mess. Months before, Bob and I had decided it might be best if we separated, at least for awhile. He had moved out of our Government Hill home and rented a small apartment in downtown Anchorage. Now I felt our situation had to be settled one way or another. I had to have some clear idea of where I was headed.

But I was too plain tired at the moment for any more bickering and arguments. I decided I would take a long-overdue trip. I wanted something more than just a short R & R. I was determined I was going to take my time and get to see new and different places and have the chance to meet new people.

My job with NANA Security came to an end just three days before the oil started to flow in the pipeline. On June 17, they deadheaded a plane to Galbraith Airport to fly me and the other remaining NANA guards to Fairbanks. At the airport in Fairbanks, I said my final good-byes and caught a regular Wien Airline flight to Anchorage and my home. That ended my more than two years in the Arctic with NANA, but although I didn't know it at the time, it wasn't to be the end of my work in the Arctic.

Once I got home, I hardly bothered to unpack my clothes. Instead, I spent a couple of days seeing some old friends, making plans and getting reservations for what would be my first long solo trip. In less than a week, I was on my way.

The first leg was a flight to Honolulu. Arriving in Hawaii, I found a room in a modest hotel in Waikiki and set out to do some exploring. I never got in the water or even visited the beach. My time was spent wandering around Waikiki seeing the sights and doing a lot of window shopping. I also made some modest purchases of warm-weather clothes and located a small travel agency that specialized in travel and tours to and in Australia.

The older gentleman at the agency had a very British accent and seemed to know everything there was to know about Australia. Bob and I had often talked in the past about one day visiting the "Down Under" continent, which appealed to me far more than anyplace I might visit. It sounded a lot like Alaska – a huge area with a very small population – but with a very different landscape and climate.

In a couple of visits with my new British friend, we laid out what I had in mind. It would be a month-long visit to what should be the most interesting spots. I wanted to make it as a one-person tour, traveling by bus but not part of a tour group.

My travel expert came up with a complete plan. It included visits to the cities of Sydney and Adalaide and to such outback spots as Alice Springs, Ayer's Rock and Coober Pedy. I also asked that it be on an inexpensive rather than a luxury basis. (Boy, he sure held to that!). What he came up with was a tour as it would be taken by an Australian rather that a rich American. Some of the accommodations were to prove almost too spartan.

So my few days in Hawaii flew by, and almost before I knew it, I was aboard a giant Quantas airliner headed for a new adventure. Landing in Sydney, I had some difficulty, but finally located my small hotel. This was my first solo visit to a big city, and it was all rather overwhelming. But I threw myself on the mercy of an Aussie taxi-driver and he delivered me to the front door of what turned out to be a "Women only" hotel run by the Salvation Army!

My room proved to be on the small side and equipped with just the bare necessities. It made my old pipeline barracks room seem like a luxury suite. However, it made no difference. The three days I spent in Sydney, I visited the room only to sleep. I spent the time I had seeing what appealed to me: the very modernistic Sydney Opera House, the Royal Botanic Garden with its display of exotic plant life, and the Taronga Zoo, where I marveled at the kangaroos, the wallabies, and the Tasmanian Devil. In all it was a good introduction, but I was eager to be on my way.

My first tour bus trip took me on to Adelaide. That was rather the low point of my trip. It wasn't Adelaide's fault, but despite its many fine old buildings and homes, to me it was just another city. After just one extra day there, I re-boarded the bus and headed for Coober Pedy and the outback.

We traveled almost 800 miles to the north and inland into the hilly desert country in the interior. As we approached our destination, our driver told us:

"We're coming into Coober Pedy, which is the Opal capital of the world!"

It was a strange and unworldly place. It was like no other place I had ever seen: Many of the homes and commercial buildings were dug out of the hillsides and actually below ground level. This to compensate for the hellish hot weather in the Australian summer when temperatures get up as high as 116 degrees. The town was surrounded by mine diggings where men labored in search of the precious opal gem stones for which it was world famous.

Aside from its strange dugout homes, the little town (some 2,000 residents) seemed to have quite a cosmopolitan air with many nationalities represented for a community out in the middle of nowhere. In that respect, it reminded me somewhat of Rock Springs, Wyoming, also a mining town and where we had lived when we were first married.

THE PLACE WHERE I stayed – it was more of a guest house than a hotel – was one of the dugouts. In addition to guest rooms, it included a cafe and even a bar, all of them with the constant cool temperature of the underground. It was an odd feeling to live and sleep in such a place.

There were also all sorts of stores in the various dugouts including, of course, jewelry stores with displays of the beautiful opals which gave Coober the reason for its establishment. I spent time touring the stores and even an underground church. I also took a bus tour to some of the opal mining properties that dotted the desert landscape surrounding the town. The opals they produced were beautiful and tempting but not something that could fit into my budget.

The opals – or one in particular – was the basis for my one unpleasant experience in Coober Pedy.

As I was coming out of an underground jewelry store, a short, dark-haired, middle-aged man approached me and asked if I was interested in opals. I told him "Yes" but that I certainly didn't have the kind of money to buy them. He then launched into a long, involved story about how he had been a miner himself until he became ill, but how he had been able to smuggle out one beautiful stone. He said he would sell the stone to me for a below-market price. I could take it back to "the States" and make myself a lot of money.

The guy looked and acted more like a used-car salesman than a former miner. I didn't want to be rude, but I told him in no uncertain terms that I was not interested and had no money to spend on opals. I thought I had brushed him off, but he turned up again during my stay. Aside from him, my time in Coober was very nice. I met several Cooberites who were very friendly and pleasant. They seemed to be as interested in my tales of Arctic Alaska as I was in what they had to tell me about life in their hellishly hot and dry desert country. What they had to say made me determined to spend more time in the future in the Australian outback.

But the Opal Guy did show up time and again. I got to where I peeked out of the front before leaving the guest house. I thought sure every time he would be lurking nearby. He apparently had it firmly fixed in his mind that I was a typical American with lots of money to spare. It finally got so bad that I complained to the guest house manager. He apologized and said he would "have a word." And amazingly it worked. I never saw the Opal Guy again!

I spent a whole week in Coober and had a fine time once the Opal Guy vanished. The folks I met there all thought, as a visitor, I should continue on north and see the town of Alice Springs and also the nearby Ayers

Rock. They said they were tourist must-sees in that part of Australia. So I finally made my bus reservations, said my good-byes and started on toward the desert center of the continent. We traveled for what seemed hours through the dry, sandy desert and when the beautiful green grass and tropical trees of Alice Springs showed on the horizon ahead, it really looked like a mirage.

What it was, of course, was an actual oasis right in the middle of the red desert. The springs, for which the town was named, had given birth to the tiny settlement and its central location gave it its growth as a road and rail hub midway between the southern and northern coasts. It had become a city of some 25,000 and an important tourist stop.

I booked into a modest hotel (prices were quite a bit higher here) for a couple of days for a look around. At first glance it didn't appeal. Much too touristy. But I took in the usual sights and I was most impressed of all with the strings of camels trudging though the sand of the then-dry Todd River and carrying their loads of tourists.

After a couple of days, I was ready to move on. I did do a bit of shopping first and equipping myself with a light day pack, a couple of quart water bottles, and a big-brimmed white hat. I figured if I was going to be traveling in the desert I had better be ready for it. Then I made my bus reservations on to Ayers Rock. I would arrive late in the day, spend the next day taking in the sights, and return to Alice the next day.

The huge reddish rock formation sitting out by itself in the desert is an impressive sight. The rock is supposedly sacred to the local native people. As we got closer, I could see a wooden walkway with handrails going up one side clear to the top. On the walkway were a number of ant-like figures – tourists struggling to the top. It came to mind: If it was a sacred place why did they let people crawl all over it? It didn't seem like something I wanted to do.

I decided that in the morning, instead of climbing the rock, I would just take a hike around it. Equipped with my big hat, lots of sunscreen, my pack and two full water bottles, that's just what I did.

The next morning dawned warm and sunny with a cloudless sky. (It really seemed that was the every-day rule in this part of Australia.) By 8:00 a.m. I had gathered my gear and left the room to start my hike around the base of the huge rock formation. I had forgotten to wear my wristwatch, but I must have trudged through the sand for a good three hours, going at a good clip, before I came to realize there was no way I was going to make it all the way around. Wearily I hiked back to my motel room.

I had failed to make it around the rock, but I had learned a couple of things. One was that Ayers Rock is a heck of a lot bigger than it seemed at first glance. The other was that the sun here was a heck of a lot stronger than the sun in Alaska. Despite all the sunscreen, I ended up with a case of sunburn on my face and arms. After taking a long, cool shower, I decided to spend the rest of the day in the shade. I took advantage of the leisure time to make my reservation back to Alice and plan out the rest of my trip.

Chapter 16

MY ORIGINAL PLAN HAD BEEN to jump on another bus in Alice and continue on north to the little crossroads community of Tennant Creek. I'd heard a lot about Tennant while in Coober Pedy. It seemed that gold was discovered there in the 1920s and shortly, they had a regular old gold rush. It all sounded like a latter-day re-run of the Klondike, and that made me want to get a look at the place.

Now, however, I was having second thoughts. The vacation month I had promised myself, was running out and I did want to spend a little more time in Hawaii on my way home. I decided Tennant Creek would have to wait until another time.

When I stopped over in Honolulu, my time was limited and I never got out of the city. I still wanted to take a bus tour around the entire Island and see the less settled parts. There was one other thing, too. I had talked to a couple of women tourists in Waikiki, who were about my age. They agreed on one thing I shouldn't miss:

"You must spend a day at the Ala Moana shopping center. It's like no mall you ever saw before. It's really Huge!"

Well, that did sound like something to see. A shopping day, plus a bus tour around the entire island would put the icing on my vacation. Tennant Creek would just have to wait for my next trip.

That's just about the way it worked out. In Alice, I got a plane back to Sydney. I overnighted there at a motel by the airport and early the next morning I was aboard a Quantas airliner for the long flight to Honolulu. This time I bypassed the Waikiki tourist area and got a room in a modest hotel downtown, very close to that giant, multi-storied shopping center.

The next morning I had breakfast in one of the several cafes on the ground floor of the shopping center. I got to talking to an older Japanese woman at the next table and learned something very interesting. She was a local and lived in one of the smaller villages on the island. She told me that I could make the trip clear around the island on city buses by asking for transfers. It would mean some short waits between buses, but it sounded a lot cheaper and more interesting than going on a tourist bus charter.

Since I was in the shopping center anyway, I spent the rest of the day window shopping in the more than 100 stores on the various floors connected by escalators and very busy with locals and tourists alike. It was a different and satisfying day. I shopped myself silly and spent hardly any money.

The next day – what was to be my last day in Hawaii – I got up early, had a light breakfast at the Ala Moana, and picked up some fruit and a sandwich for my lunch. Then I boarded my first city bus right at the shopping center and set off on my island adventure. It was a very different day and I got to meet a number of local people during my four bus rides. I got to see the sugar cane fields, the fields of pineapples and the other truck farms as well as residential areas, beaches and parks, and the giant military installations. It was, in all, a very satisfying trip and made for a very long day.

164

Chapter 16

This was the end of my extended "R & R" trip. It had been a bit lonely at times but, going solo, I did get to meet a lot of interesting people. It just showed me I could do it and left me determined to do more traveling in the future – one way or the other. Now it was back to Anchorage and an attempt to straighten out my tangled personal life.

Despair

I'm sitting in my frosted-up pickup truck in a snow-filled lot on the banks of the Yukon while I turn the heater up as high as it will go to fight the chill pressing in from the sub-zero cold outside. This old GMC will be my only shelter and my home for the next 12 hours as I foot patrol back and forth across the Yukon River Bridge. As I sit here munching on a cold sandwich, I think about how ironic it is that little more than a year ago, I was staying in an underground hotel in the Australian desert town of Coober Pedy where the summer heat can get up to 116 degrees. Now, of my own doing, I am back here working out in the snow at a temperature of 12 below zero.

A whole lot had happened to me the past year to bring me back to far northern Alaska. I can't say that much of it was pleasant. I was engaged in arguments with my now ex-husband Bob first about getting a divorce and then about dividing what little property we had. At the same time I was battling some officials at the Laborers' Union local in Anchorage about my pension rights. Yes, quite a year. It seemed almost peaceful and pleasant to be back again on the line.

I came away with the feeling that Bob is no longer healthy, either mentally or physically. However, we did finally manage to agree to the terms of the divorce. I will retain title to our house in Anchorage and make the final mortgage payments. Bob will take our pickup camper and get title to our log cabin at Willow.

It was a really terrible thing to divorce a man I had been married to for nearly 30 years. The feeling was as though I had lost part of myself, an arm or leg. It still doesn't seem real, but I have to keep going. I have to find a way to go on living and making a way for myself. I have to face up to the fact that I am nearing 60 years of age, that I will probably live alone for the rest of my life, and I have to find the means to support myself for the years I have left.

In a strange turn of events, the Laborers' Union provided me with a lawyer to handle the divorce at the same time some of its officials were arguing that I would lose my pension rights if I went back to work on the pipeline with security firms which were now non-union.

Thankfully, higher officials overruled this with the result that, so long as I continued to belong to the union and paid my dues, I could go back on the job again and my hours would count toward a pension.

As a result I applied for a job with Wackenhut Security and was hired for guard duty on the northern section of the line. This in itself was a strange turn of events, as I had applied with Wackenhut back in 1975 and got brushed off. They said then that they only hired people with police experience. Apparently my 26 months with NANA changed things.

Things were very different when I got back on the line. We had different uniforms – looked more like police – and we were given firearms training and carried weapons while on duty.

I was first assigned to Prudhoe Bay, but was there only a short time before moving south to Five Mile for patrol work on the Yukon River Bridge. That's where I was sitting in my pickup between foot patrols. It was October now, and the river was iced up but not closed yet despite the sub-zero temperatures. At this time, our patrols took two different paths: One route over the bridge itself and then the other over the catwalk, which held the pipeline. Between patrols, I sit in the pickup trying to get warm again while I make one of my 15-minute radio reports.

Things here are about to change and not for the better. Tomorrow the Yukon Check Point will close, absorbed by the state. Then I will remain on bridge duty but will no longer be able to visit the check point for company or hot drinks. This old GMC will really be my one and only home while on duty.

If this post is not abolished, I will be here at least until the middle of November. Here in the pickup I will try to get warm, eat, and set out to do some patrolling. It will be a restricted and very lonely life, and I dread it, but I must go ahead with it or I will have to quit.

Staying awake will be difficult, but I suppose I can do it if I set my mind to it. Aside from radio checks every 15 minutes, I will have no contact with anyone. It will be something like voluntary solitary confinement. Knowing it will be the very, very last time I have to submit to such a detail, then it will seem a little less grim. (By the time I finish up with the bridge patrol, I should have my hours in to qualify for a pension.)

Chapter 17

TONIGHT HAS GONE WELL. It has been cold. Back at the pump station it was only 1 below zero, but out here it's steady at 12 below. It's light tonight – a big moon and mostly clear. A man who stopped at the CP said he had never seen the river so iced up at this time of year. The center channel keeps getting more and more slow. It takes a good look to see it moving at all.

The next day now, and it's Sunday, October 15. (My countdown is 27.). When I arrived at the check point, I found everybody and everything was gone. No gun. No radio. But then Barry and Walter came back to the bridge and passed along the gun and belt and the radio. This night is not too cold. There's cloud cover and the moon is hidden.

At this point, 27 more shifts seems like eternity. Can I really stand it? Is it worth it? This must be the lowest point of my entire life. If I can get over this, I can get over anything. I quit the thinking and went out and did a catwalk patrol. Came back and managed to brush my teeth.

The sergeant arrived and took me down to meet the new people at the check point: an older man – very mediocre – and a young man with bleached hair. They invited me down to drink coffee but I doubt if I go. Neither of the men appears interesting to talk to and if this is to be an "experience" I must stay out. Anyway, things are not the same with Mike gone and all.

The biggest bugaboo will be fighting sleep. Chewing gum will help some. At this moment the whole thing sounds like hell. Impossible.

The only thing I discovered that helps is the small head lamp powered by one of the big batteries. I clip this to a visor and it works beautifully. No longer is my GMC just a bottomless black pit. I can even see to read a little or write up my notes.

It's been a quiet evening for traffic. Around 11:00 p.m. I went to the checkpoint. The blonde boy was there. I had some warm tea and talked a bit – nothing interesting. Later I found my big flashlight needed batteries, so I drove to Pump Station 6 and also got a cup of good coffee. In thinking about it, I now feel Jack Knight did well to be able to stay on the Tanana River crossing for two years. This really is an awful job at night.

However, there must be a way for me to do this so that it is less painful. Plan something? Perhaps I should use the next 26 days to try to form some good habits. To be more positive. I should think no negative thoughts for 26 days and see how I feel. Is that really possible?

Actually, it's been quite pleasant tonight with the big moon out once again. There is lots of light and everything is almost as visible as in daytime. The big old river is still flowing – but very slowly. It is thick and dark like oil. Snow is starting slowly, visible in the glare of the diesel floodlights. I'd just as soon not see any more snow.

When the sergeant was down, I asked him about getting a light in the pickup. He was absolutely no help. He said:

"Just use your flashlight. That's all you need to write up your log. That's all I used to use."

But, Sarge, what about the times when you are stopped? (I didn't ask him this, I just thought it.) You can't be driving all the time, and when you are stopped you need a bit of light and a few minutes to relax. If you just have to sit in the dark all the time, that is the route to ulcers and madness. (Thank God I thought to get that extra head lamp and big battery.)

After the sergeant's visit and all, I finished up the shift feeling very low and hopeless. As far as I can see, there is no way I can ever get my life squared around. Mostly its my own fault, and now at this stage, what can I do? In any event, it's too late. Much too late.

MY NEXT SHIFT WAS better, and I started to feel somewhat optimistic again. Maybe there was something of a future for me. It was a mild evening to start out. Some 10 to 13 above, and I didn't feel as sleepy as the past couple of nights. I had bought a *Fairbanks News-Miner* and enjoyed reading it between my hikes. My little light on the visor is quite good and provides enough light to read and write by. Perhaps I should have Don Mullen order some more bulbs, just in case.

Time has gone relatively fast. I wrote one letter–to Bette. About 2:00 a.m. I went up for gas and a radio battery, and talked for a few minutes with Paul. He said Robert McCarter is taking Dick's place as sergeant.

There's been no moon tonight, too cloudy. But it's been a very pleasant evening and night – already I've adjusted and find this not half bad. It's lonely, yes, but mixing in a little pleasure such as reading and writing makes time go faster. I've walked nine miles tonight and it's almost time now to take the last lap. The wind has risen, but the chill factor is not as bad as before. Or maybe the cocoa and cookie I had helped keep me warm.

Just before midnight, a trucker stopped by and said hello. He offered to get me anything in town that I want. He is the one with the fantastic gold nugget and ruby necklace. Also manicured nails. Apparently quite a ladies' man, but decent enough.

The next day my count was down to 25, but the weather had gone sour. The little storm on my last shift had turned into a great, big, roaring storm. By the time I started work in the evening, the snow was coming down hard without a let-up. To make matters worse, there was a considerable wind behind it. My trail to the catwalk had completely drifted over. When I started down there, I was plowing through snow up to my knees. Oh, for a broom!

The sergeant stopped by for a minute, and I assured him I was okay. It is not really cold, which is a blessing. By the early morning hours the wind is stopped and being outside is pleasant. The snow was still coming down but not so hard.

I wrote to Inez, my Government Hill neighbor, and finished a letter to Bette. I had several deck walks – and these were pleasant – the river is terrific. There are great pads of ice surrounded by countless small, round ones. (I learned later this is called "pancake" ice, and each piece is neatly round as a pancake.)

On Wednesday it was snowing like a son-of-a-gun when I drove to work. The temperature is very mild. I am extremely depressed most of the shift. I can see no way things can get better for me. As Alma told me, they can only get worse as you grow older. I cannot jump in the river – something prevents me. But I have been divorced twice now – you could say two men have dumped me so what good would it do to find another? Yet, if I don't have a husband or a lover, what do I have? How do I get over this devastating loneliness?

Unfortunately, my whole life was built around my marriage. The only answer is to find a place and something to do that will keep me absorbed. And soon. Such crushing hopelessness cannot last long because I will soon perish from it.

I realize that being here alone in the cold and dark is bad for me. But knowing that doesn't make anything easier. There is just nothing to write about this evening. Just the dark, cold hopelessness.

It was still snowing the next day, but not so much. No wind and warm temperature. I went to the medic's (Tom Wilson) to look at his new slides. They were taken with a 28mm lens on a Canon. Quite good. They were sunset photos where he used color filters, turning the sunset blood red. A striking effect but perhaps too much.

Again, it was a dull evening at the bridge. My despondency increases. Or at least it doesn't decrease. My whole life has been such a mess – all was wrong from the beginning. Why? I had a lot going for me: smart, reasonably attractive, ambitious, capable, industrious. But everything eluded me. Why? Why? So much of what happened between Bob and me was my fault. I knew it then; I know it now.

The days of darkness and cold stretch ahead endlessly. Then I will be home. I wonder if I will be happy for a few days.

IT'S SNOWING AGAIN on Friday and a mild 19 degrees. They say a new sergeant is on the way from Fairbanks. Dick has left. That's a blessing because he had lost all interest. He certainly had none in my welfare. He thought I should sit here in the darkness with just a flashlight to write in the log. He was a real charlatan. He thought if you were miserable you would work better. Or maybe he just hated everyone who worked for him.

My morale is now sky high (almost). I met the new sergeant when I went to the messhall for some fruit. He seemed really interested in the work and just a nice guy. Then, this afternoon, I received the package from Millie with the insulated pants, Sorel shoe pacs and insulated socks. Great. So this is no longer a worry. I wore the shoes to work and it made a lot of difference. Now my feet are very cozy and warm. It makes me feel warm all over.

Sergeant McCarter visited me at the bridge and things looked even better. He is going to see that I have a light in the pickup. He appears very interested and enthusiastic, a vast contrast to what I have seen since going on this bridge. He'll be down again tomorrow night to hike the catwalk with me. Then to cap things off, Jim Bishop came down with a new battery for my light. Terrific. Things are definitely looking up!

Chapter 17

Now it's Sunday again, and I feel extremely tired. I could hardly drag myself out of bed, even at 3:00 p.m., which is late. Then never did get really rolling – just dragged. I wondered if I'd even be able to get to work. However, after I'd eaten, I felt better. The sergeant stopped by and talked. He told me about his wife and son. A very pleasant man. We did not go on the catwalk.

The next morning we were hit by a bad storm. The temperature dropped to minus 4, and the wind was blowing a steady 20 mph with some higher gusts. With the wind chill factor, that made the actual temperature 35 below zero. "Remember, be careful out there!"

I had figured it was way down and dressed for it. I was extra warmly dressed in my new insulated gear. I had on both parkas, shoe pacs with insulated innersole, new insulated socks, and the earflaps down on my mouton hat. I passed the evening in relative comfort. But the intense cold does make for hard going. It's very tiring.

Near the end of my shift when I came to the pickup, there was a martin playing around there. He crawled up on the snow berm and looked at the car and lights quizzically. I made an extra vehicle patrol and my replacement came down to the north end to take the radio and gun. When I came up to the bridge there was the martin lying dead. Whether I ran over him, or my replacement did, I do not know, but it made me very sad. He was an engaging little fellow with round ears and pretty brown fur.

On Tuesday, my count was down to 18. It was quite pleasant on shift with a temperature above zero and no wind. It also helps now that I have the cozy shoe pacs. Guard Paul Hesch came down and made the rounds with me. Nothing unusual or extraordinary about the night.

I did receive two rolls of color film today from the camera store. I had sent for it in September and it took six weeks to arrive! I also sent for information on Havasu City. Bette has been talking it up. I must get some direction in my life and perhaps the best place to start is finding out where I really want to live, or at least spend most of my time. I also had another letter from Bette really reading me off for continuing to stay up here. And I know I am wrong.

THE NEXT FEW DAYS were mild and continuing snow. The shifts were uneventful and my journal was mostly blank except for a complaint about "cops and robbers" stuff with the security company. I felt very discouraged about the whole thing – working conditions. And then my health started to decline.

On October 27, it was still snowing and with enough breeze to make it miserable. Early in the shift I found I had a slight cold and my nose was running, some bleeding from my nose and considerable sneezing. I finally decide it is more from dryness of my respiratory tract rather than a cold. I hung some wet paper towels in the pickup and also tried breathing steam from the Thermos. It is a miserable condition, especially in the outdoors on patrol. However, I am feeling okay otherwise so I am able to keep working.

But then my wen started acting up. I am going to have to go in and see Doctor Fish when I go home. I hate to quit before the regular R & R.

The next day it is still snowing and windy. I have to wear the red parka under the green one. Very nasty. To make matters worse, my wen was swollen ,and I was not feeling too hot. I felt very perturbed by all this and what seems to be my failing health. Fortunately it was a quiet and uneventful night.

When I woke the next day the wen was very sore. I decided I would have to go see the medic. I hate to get a full exam, but I may have to. When I go he says it is a cyst – and calls it by name. We decided I would soak in his office tub when I get off, and again when I get up. In very hot water. At least he will send me on medical if I have to go to Fairbanks. That will help, I think.

I have an exceedingly rotten feeling tonight. Very sore. I walk as little as possible; sit still as much as possible. I made all the basic rounds, but nothing extra. I feel almost like I have the flu – I ache all over. I wonder if it's poison from the wen. It's really difficult to stay on the job. My whole existence is at a very, very low ebb at this time.

The sergeant came down to the pickup with news of a bad wind storm in Anchorage. He stayed while I went up and called Inez, my neighbor on Boyd Street, to see if my house was okay. She said all is well despite winds up to 137 mph!

The night drags because I have to spend so much time just sitting. On one trip I see dozens of animal tracks crossing the road in new snow. Wolves? Foxes?

Some of the tracks seem large. Nearing the parking space I see a martin galloping down the middle of the road. They're his tracks, alright. The rascal darts off, and then returns right in front of the pickup. Fortunately, I am able to miss him. They move strangely – galloping is the only word. For such a small animal it is a funny gait. They do not move as fast as I would think. Cute little guys, though.

At the end of my shift I have to drag myself to my room and bed. I sure hope and pray that I can stay and that the wen gets better.

THE NEXT MORNING I was grounded by the Medic. It's my first "day off" since I have been working on the line. He examined the wen and it is now an awful sight. No wonder I hurt at work last night. The Medic extracted a shiny white object like an out-sized white-head. He had to lance the wound – it hurt like hell! If that dumb Doctor hadn't said "Wait" this would not have happened. Now I'm really in a pickle. I had no idea it might react this way. I had to just loaf all day, after taking a hot bath. The indignity and sorrow and beastliness of being a woman! Right now I just hate myself and my body!

That was the low point. By the next day I was feeling much better, although not well yet. The place is still sore. Urinating is painful since it gets in the wound. I'm taking penicillin – had a shot today and also pills. I will have to be very careful on my shift tonight. I'll probably go down to the porta-potty.

It turns out that it is a nice night. About 12 degrees and still. In just one night's time the river has changed dramatically. A whole section of skin has formed between the northern and the next supports of the bridge. The floating cells of ice have anchored from the shore out and now are totally still. The floes are truly like cells –now hooked together into a sort of skin. Around the edge of this quiet mass is a raised ledge or fence – not high but very visible. Only the very center of the river is flowing fast. Toward the south shore, the water is clogged with cells – still moving and sounding precisely like a river of ice cubes. I must get down to see this during the day. Soon. Perhaps Tom the Medic would like to come along.

By the next day I am feeling even better. The cyst wound is less inflamed and looking as if it might be going to grow its own skin. The soreness in my groin is becoming less. I'm on the way back!

It's very mild outside. It must be 20 degrees. All of the big Alyeska Security enchiladas are coming in tomorrow to stay all night. Oh, wow! I must wash in the a.m. and look sharp. But how sharp can one look in these clothes and working outside? Well, I will try. But warmth comes before sharpness.

I have my own pickup with light now! Great.

Last night and tonight I went to the Check Point and had coffee and used the porta-potty. I think the older man, Skip, who works there, has the "hots" for me. What an old asshole. While talking about R & R, he asked where I would spend mine. I said at home in Anchorage. He said, oh, he had thought if it was Fairbanks, we might get together. Then I mentioned Willow and the possibility I might move there after I left the line. So he said:

"Let's me and you go live at Willow."

Oh, the hideous idea of being that close to that stupid, ugly man! He has a big belly and is really gross looking. And no education. What would he see about me that would even give him the faintest idea I am a prospect for him? My age? Or does he have such an ego that he considers himself suitable for *anyone?* No doubt the latter. Men tend to think they are irresistible just for being men. Not to me they aren't! Ick! I will not stop by again. The very idea makes me ill.

It appeared things were going to be active on my next shift. There were two wrecks – one north, one south. A man pinned under a pickup to the south, to the north, an oil spill. Blimp Anne comes out and tells me all this as I go to work. Why?

Doyle, the pump station manager, told me at dinner they are trying to get rid of Anne. They dislike her. I don't know why. Walt said all the big enchiladas left. Good! Walt's a pretty nice guy, despite always sleeping in. He dislikes Anne – says she's too pushy and bossy. Still, she gets to do far more than I do: overtime, field work. I wonder if they are afraid to send me? Or is it just that I'm not available? I have begun to despise night work.

They sent me to the check point to say the road south is now clear. That sickening Skip asked me to have coffee. I said, no, thanks, and went on my way. The lieutenant stopped and talked. He's too slick for me to really like, though I do like him better than the last one.

I can't say any of this outfit thrills me. It's all very different from NANA. Smart Ass Mike said they are quite military, which is what Alyeska wants, and that is why NANA lost out and they won.

The lieutenant said I had nothing to worry about coming back. If I can just get in one or two more tours, that is *It!* That much I know. (He also commented on the good luck they had with female guards. He feels they stick with their jobs best, adjust better than men because "they are used to waiting." He says that's a female characteristic. Maybe too, I think to myself, it's because not many good-paying jobs are open to women. You stand what you have to.)

Friday was really a bad day. Walt (the day guard), just didn't show up. Nobody said "boo" and there I sat. All very depressing, but I can't just leave and desert the post. Finally at almost 7:00 a.m. Walt arrived. He tried to feed me a line about his watch being wrong. I was disgusted. I took the radio and gun off and just drove up. No time to soak. Had breakfast in my room.

When I came to work next day, the sergeant was at the north end of the bridge. I told him I was very upset because Ann, Paul, and Walt were just "using me." Now Walt has gone on R & R, thank God.

The sergeant took some photos in the light glare near the parking area —color. We will also take some black and whites. For *my* purposes. But he doesn't know that.

This job is really getting me down – the military flavor. Tonight the sergeant told me I had to stop at the gate on the way out. That means meeting the blimp. Oh well, I can stand anything for a week. But it's rough going. Can I really stand three more months? Is the money worth it? I must quit bringing up Mike Dullen as a good person to work with. The sergeant doesn't like that. I can tell. Oh to be free – free – free. No more police or military types telling me what to do when. Hold yourself in, Willie, don't blow it now.

ON SATURDAY WE had another mild evening. It was 1 below zero but it felt warmer. There was no wind or bite to the air. The new man relieved me early. He seems quite nice, but I'm still suffering from all that happened yesterday. I find that hurt feelings take longer to heal out here, just like a skin wound.

I made what is to be my daily stop at the guard shack. Unfortunately, my looks mirror my feelings, and the sergeant remarked about my not wanting to stop. This is not strictly so. I have no deep feelings about it. Perhaps just a feeling of an invasion of privacy, above and beyond all that has already been foisted upon me. Now I must leave even earlier and have less time to eat. My stomach rebels at both the food and the haste in eating. I feel slightly nauseated most of the time. My cyst area is still slightly swollen and tender, but it has not given me any troubles.

I have to note here, that I feel as if, in order to stay on the job, I have been pulling something tangible and real out of my interior. Every day I reach down and pull out a little more – and go off to work. And there isn't much left. I can tell that. I'm beginning to feel empty.

Chapter 17

How many times now have I made the trip under the bridge? Most times I've been unafraid. Now, as in the beginning, I search the lighted area for whatever might be lurking. Bears? Wolves? Tonight, I thought I saw a dozen wolves. Wolves probably would not attack, but I have the feeling they would be terrifying, just crowding around me. Sticky with curiosity.

The sergeant says he is looking into a state plane to Fairbanks for my R & R. I suppose the plane would be best, although a ride out by truck (like the male guards get) would be fun and unusual. But I shall say nothing. Morale in camp is a bit low, for some reason.

How can I possibly stand this for five more days? But I don't have much choice, do I?

On Tuesday Tom the Medic stopped by. We had a long chat about this and that. He's quite interesting. He sees much that many other men don't. I gave him some tea and a check ($45) for analysis of the cyst. It would be fun to sit down with plenty of time to talk. I think I'd get a lot out of it. Also Glenn Gibson, who came down the river in a sailboat, stopped by for supper.

Tonight I noticed that, for the most part, the ice movement of the Yukon has stopped. No movement was visible. In the center, around the two middle supports, movement like huge ice cubes rushing beneath the solid top layer, could be heard. At midnight this was still audible. But when I made my last patrol between 5:15 and 5:45, this sound was gone. All was silent – no sound save the generators on the rack.

So in these few hours, the Yukon has finally been stilled. Perhaps for the next six months. The long winter sleep.

ONLY TWO MORE GET-UPS! It's Wednesday, November 8 and the night I disgraced myself. I failed to answer my radio. It had been turned down in my pocket and I just failed to think of the time check. The worst thing about this was the presence of the lieutenant. Perhaps he'll fire me. I was sitting here at the north end of the bridge with my bright light on, reading. Oh horrors. Paul actually got here and I didn't even see him until he was here. This light is a trap.

There were no journal notes for the next two days. Even long after I left the bridge, I recalled how near to collapse I was at this point in both mind and body. Ten weeks on the Yukon River Bridge patrol was just too much.   Part of that time was before snow fell, but the really difficult time was after the snowfalls and in the bad weather and wind. I crawled around the bridge, clad in two parkas and heavy shoe pacs and a gun nearly as big as I was. Not to mention a handheld radio and a flashlight.

I made six full roundtrips on foot seven nights a week. The bridge is a half-mile long. That meant a full trip on the catwalk, down below the bridge, on the deck, and on the rack alongside, crawling from one to the other on slippery metal rungs. One round each was the minimum, often I made two.

The only reason I was sent out on R & R at that time was through the kindness of Sergeant McCarter.

The lieutenant objected to my going out, but McCarter insisted and had his way in the end. Why he objected we never knew.

Saturday, November 11 was a national holiday and a mighty big day for me too. I was all packed up and ready to go, and Sergeant McCarter had a pickup waiting for me to drive on out. I started right after an early breakfast on no sleep for 20 hours. It was a grueling and brutal trip even had I been rested, as it's 160 miles over icy, unpaved roads in the dead of winter. But you do what you have to do.

I stopped once for coffee at Sam's Place in Livengood to keep me awake. Of course, I made it into Fairbanks okay. There was no problem driving, except for extreme tiredness. My niece, Millie Saunders picked me up at the point where I left the pickup (some warehouse, as I recall). So I said goodbye to the Yukon River Bridge and I was ready for a good, long rest.

"The Job"
and the End of the Line

Looking back now on the time I spent on "the job" in the northern sub-zero country, it's really hard for me to weigh up the good and the bad. I ask myself: Did I just waste some four years of my life for no good reason? Or did those years result in some kind of benefit? As far as my personal life goes, I really can't feel I am as well off as I was four years ago. Of course, I ended up with considerably more money than when I started, but at the same time my marriage was apparently lost in the process.

It's a funny thing how that "big money" meant so many different things to the people who worked on the line. Just what made folks join in the old-time gold rushes, or in modern times get a job on the pipeline? It was, of course, the idea of "striking it rich." But there was usually something else too. I have said that money was my biggest interest. But money was not the only factor. There were many who needed the money more than I but never had any idea of going to work on the line.

No, after long and careful reflection, I decided it was no more just the idea of great riches that prompted my determination to get my job than it was only such a dream that made people all over the world head for the Klondike gold fields. There was something more: The

186

idea of a completely new and different life and the hope that it would all be a great adventure. Perhaps the last such adventure.

Well, it did turn out to be an adventure of sorts – although one that was mixed with a great deal of routine work and boredom. As to a new and different life, that certainly proved true, particularly for those of us who worked on the far northern Arctic portion of the pipeline.

Those camps north of the Yukon River were such a different deal than the ones to the south. South of the Yukon, the camps were located at or near large or small civilian communities. These included Livengood, Fairbanks, Delta Junction, Glennallen, and Valdez. But at the Arctic camps we were virtually in prison in the wilderness. There was no way to get rid of steam except to work. That was one of the big reasons so many people almost fell apart before R & R.

Actually, the psychological aspect of working in the Arctic and living in a remote camp I found the most fascinating of any facet of this life. I found that sooner or later, just about everyone came across a moment when he or she was stopped dead in their tracks by a cold and very disconcerting thought:

"What in God's name am I doing here?"

That was, no doubt, the very moment when many people quit; those three out of five that could not stand the life. That critical moment didn't account for all three, but a good portion. Some few, of course, got fired or left for some other reason. But just imagine – the turnover was three in five! Not a few got only as far as the airport (coming in) and either waited for the next plane or wouldn't get off the one they were on.

This restricted life in the Arctic camps was made even more restricted for us security guards. We were expected to "set an example" for the other workers. There were no parties for us or getting together with people outside of the security ranks. Even my off-duty hours were strictly regulated. Mentioning, one nice day, that I was going to take a walk out on the tundra, got me the reminder that I had to sign out anytime I went outside the camp limits. I had to state where I was going and why and the time I would be back in camp.

"You must report if you go walking – in case you have an accident."

At that point I was beginning to see why so many people in those camps took to drink. They had this feeling of being crushed, watched and so on that is just shattering. Yes, it was something like being in a prison.

Just about everyone felt that way at one time or another. For instance, one morning at Galbraith I was having coffee when Ray Leach came in and sat and talked for a long time, even though he was on duty. I mentioned Ray a time or two earlier: He was an older man (62) who had been a bandmaster in the navy and was an accomplished musician. Ray seemed very upset and unsure about his job.

THIS WAS A CURIOUS SITUATION, but not at all unusual. There were some very insecure people in command and they made it difficult for others. I could see where the majority of us might need to sit down and talk from time to time and get a boost so we could continue working. I told Ray that I had made up my mind I was not going to worry about the job in any way – I would do my best and if that proved not enough, well it was just too bad.

It is always surprising to find someone – who seems calm and well-adjusted – not to be precisely the way they seem. I ended up trying to assure Ray that he is liked and respected and hoped that he felt better. The job at Galbraith was probably his last chance to save up some money. He had the same intentions as I had – to make this one last stake. At the time he and his wife, Ruthie, had been married 39 years.

To my mind, it wasn't older people like Ray (and myself) who were the problem on the job. Rather it was the real young men who came wanting the money but not willing to do the work to earn it.

While I was still working at Galbraith, we got a new guard who was a young kid from Montana. He had been working as a guard at Five Mile for Bechtel and left to come to this job because it paid more money. I had a hunch he wasn't going to like it or to last very long. The first night he made the rounds with Warren and then with me. Even before we finished my round, he was complaining about his back and about how tired he was. I thought to myself just wait until he gets into the boring end of this thing and it will be more than his back hurting. I was right he didn't last long.

Warren himself was another example of what I was talking about with the problems with the young men on the job. He would much rather be curled up with a book in some out-of-the-way spot than making the rounds checking furnaces. The story was that his one qualification for the job was that his father was a judge in Fairbanks. True? I didn't know.

What do I remember most from my years on the job? First of all I would have to say the tens of thousands of furnace checks I had to make on foot patrol. Then came all of the fire alarms that I had to investigate. While they mostly turned out to be be false, I vividly remember the two or three that were the real thing. Most of all I remember the one I answered while on foot patrol in the middle of a cold night at Happy Valley. I still get chills remembering my running frantically through the barracks to wake everyone and get them to safety.

The wildlife in our Arctic wilderness area also comes to mind. Particularly, of course, the numerous times we had to herd grizzly bears trying to visit camp. And then there was the two-legged variety of wildlife I encountered from time to time such as the Undershorts Desperado. (By the way, that guy came to a bad end. Some time after I left Galbraith, I heard he was once again caught walking around in his underwear in the women's barracks, and was fired and escorted off the line.)

MAYBE MOST OF ALL though, my mind replays the just plain beauty of that Arctic area with the towering, snow-covered mountains of the Brooks Range and the endless grass and moss of the tundra. The two seasons each had their own kinds of beauty. The long, harsh winter was some times hard to take, but it offered clear, sharp views of distant, snowy peaks and, at times, the odd beauty of the ice fog that covered all objects and gave them an unworldly look. By contrast, much of the beauty of the brief but brilliant summer was in the tundra that bloomed in multi-colored wildflowers.

Those are all the kinds of things that come to mind, but they don't answer the basic question: Were those years just a waste of my time? Or did all that work have some real benefit? Ever since I got back from the line, I have been trying to weigh up the good and the bad of that experience.

I guess you would have to say that one of the plus factors of my job were all of the many and varied people I met while walking all those foot patrols. It was certainly a mighty cross-section of folks, male and female, younger and older, from many places around the world and of many nationalities. That was a worthwhile experience and one I would never have had if I had stayed at home.

I hope that at least some of the many friendships I made while on the line will carry over to civilian life. I'd like to see Eric and Roger again sometime and to see how they are doing nowadays. I'd also like to get together with Ray Leach and his wife wife, Ruthie. Most of all, I would like to be able to continue my friendship with Jean, my long-time roommate.

In a special category of the people I think about from pipeline days, is my niece, Millie Saunders. She wasn't actually working on the pipeline at the time I started my job. But she did go later to join her husband, Bud. As I think I mentioned earlier, Millie was the daughter of my half-sister, Alma Moore, and she was born in 1932 while Alma was living at Dayville, Oregon.

She married Buddy Dean Saunders in 1948, and they lived in a number of places from California to Alaska over the years as they raised a family of three children and Bud worked in the construction industry.

At the time I was looking for a pipeline job, they had a home in Fairbanks. Bud was already working on the line, and Millie had a job as a secretary at the Laborers' Union local office. To say that Millie helped me look for a job would be the understatement of the year. Then, while I was on the line, she helped in so many ways by sending me needed supplies and providing transportation when I was in Fairbanks on R & R. I have to give Millie special thanks.

After the friendships that I made on the line, I would have to say that the next biggest benefit to me was the chance to really see and admire that strange and wonderful Arctic country. Even the chance to work in the often sub-zero cold was a new experience and a chance to test your stamina. Right?

Last, but of course not least, on the good side of the ledger was the opportunity to amass the funds to insure retirement. This included the small but worthwhile union pension and health insurance.

I have already made mention some of the items on the minus side: The breakup of my marriage and, you might say, the loss of four of the years I have left. I think you also have to include the fact that working on the line made me more cynical about life in general. Then too, there was the utter boredom that you had to battle so much of the time while on patrol. I'll also add having to put up with the "police" mentality – the suspicion and the distrust of each and everyone.

So that's the balance sheet – the good and the bad. How does it add up? It's still really hard for me to tell. Maybe it will take me years to decide if it was all worthwhile. Or, maybe I never will be able to decide. For now the jury is still out.

I've been going through all the journals I kept day by day for the years I was on the job. I think my present attitude toward the whole thing was best summed up in an entry I made while we were on the re-badging expedition.

This was Christmas time in 1975. We had spent Christmas eve working at Prospect and then drove on to Coldfoot on Christmas Day. I had written a letter to Bob and said:

> I am finding out how good we have had it all these years and how much I would miss you if we have to spend our time apart. Today is just about meaningless. And Christmas Eve – just like coming home and finding your home stripped. I guess it's been a good experience for me, but it's certainly a sad one. . .

Then I went on, noting that Coldfoot wasn't the worst place to spend the holiday if you had to spend it alone. I noted that the camp, in the southern foothills of the Brooks Range, was in a beautiful spot:

It's a nicely arranged camp, and for a wonder they left the trees – lots of them around the barracks. Squirrels too. But it's so quiet now. I will go to dinner about 6:00 p.m. There doesn't seem to be any sound in the whole camp. There's no hilarious parties – none at all – that I can hear.

Oh, for an eggnog. . .

AFTERWORD

When Wilma finally left the Yukon River Bridge and ended her pipeline years, my obsession with the magazine was still in full bloom. After some twelve years as editor, I was still putting in extra long hours, six and seven days week and with really very little to show for it. I was being treated for depression by a psychiatrist and it seemed I was just about living on tranquilizers.

Then, just a few months later, things changed suddenly. One Saturday, I had a complete mental and physical collapse. My doctor got me admitted to Providence Hospital and I spent a week there. It was a week that helped me to change my entire outlook on life. I finally realized that working at the magazine wasn't really the most important thing in my life. Wilma actually came to visit me almost every day that week, and she was my only visitor.

I never went back to the magazine. In fact, I never even set foot in the magazine office again. When I left the hospital, I moved up to our log cabin near Willow. I spent most of the winter there alone, except for a cat that wandered in one day and stayed to keep me company. (The magazine changed hands a few months after I left, and a year later it ceased publication.)

Early the next year I started work in a new job. A statewide non-profit agency for senior citizens, funded by the state and federal governments, had a small house organ published by volunteers that they wanted to turn into a senior newspaper distributed throughout Alaska. They advertised a job opening for a reporter and I applied. After being interviewed, it turned out that what they really wanted was an editor to turn the house organ into a statewide *Senior Voice.* I was hired as editor and turned around and hired one of the other applicants to be my lone reporter.

What I found I needed most in the new job was someone who knew the business and knew me, and could help me plan out the new publication. Rather naturally, I turned to Wilma, and we spent many hours plotting out the paper's future. She came up with the idea that despite government funding, the paper should seek advertising support to pay at least part of its way. She also volunteered to take on the job of advertising manager – without pay – and to be rewarded only by commissions on what she sold.

Her plan worked. Soon she had to hire another woman to help with the sales. The paper itself grew to a larger size, with more pages. We hired a second reporter and a graphic artist, so the entire publishing process could be in-house. The *Anchorage Daily News* offered to do the press work on a non-profit basis.

During the next two years, our senior paper expanded in both reach and reportation. It was being made available to senior citizens all across Alaska, from Ketchikan to Barrow. It won a few press awards and one Fairbanks columnist described it as "the feisty little paper" that went to bat for its readers. We began to feel our job was done. The paper had been established and it was just about time for us to retire. We put the plan into motion by turning over the editorship to the reporter I had first hired. Meanwhile, we decided to spend some retirement years in Hawaii, and Wilma put the Anchorage home up for sale.

We bought a house and a half-acre on the Big Island out in the subdivisions and surrounded by jungle on all four sides. We had planned to get married again in Hawaii, but, as things happened, we actually were married by a judge in Arizona while on a trip to the mainland. Then followed what were probably the happiest and healthiest years of our lives. We spent most daylight hours outside tending the exotic plants in our yard including our banana and pineapple plants and breadfruit tree. It was a far cry from all of our years in Alaska!

One unfortunate thing was that, with two exceptions, Wilma was unable to keep up with the friends she made on the pipeline. Once the construction was completed, the workers scattered to the four winds, and she lost track of them. One exception was Dick North who achieved a certain amount of fame with the publication of two more books of Yukon history and with one of his books turned into a TV movie. He and his wife settled in Dawson and Dick took over as curator of a local museum.

The other exception was Wilma's pipeline roommate. Along with all of her other writing, Wilma was a prolific letter writer, and she kept up a correspondence with Jean, who had shared many of her pipeline experiences. During our Big Island years, Jean and her husband, Jim, came to visit us for a couple of days. Wilma and Jean spent some hours talking over their years in the Arctic. (What a setting for yarns about the frozen north!)

Years later, when island life became too confining and we moved to the mainland, Jean and Jim stopped by our home in New Mexico en route to their own new location in Florida. These chances to talk with Jean were one of the things that helped spur Wilma on in her project to write a book about her "Four Years Below Zero."

Acknowledgements

First on the list is Phil Nanzetta of Signature Book Printing Inc. who was kind enough to take on this tiny little project. He responded promptly to our every request and patiently tolerated the many questions and mistakes we made along the way.

The staff at the Anchorage Museum were very attentive and helpful in providing information and high quality scans of Wilma's photos.

The nice people at the University of Alaska, Fairbanks and Anchorage and the Alaska State Library who also assisted us in various ways.

Rhonda Saunders-Ricks, kindly furnished several background details and a photo of her mother, Millie.

Special thanks go to Lauri Sliney of Fairbanks who went out of her way to provide us with the nice photo of the E.L. Patton Bridge (aka Yukon River Bridge) and the permission to use it in this book.

Many thanks to all of you!

GLOSSARY

ARCO - The Atlantic Richfield Corporation made the first discovery of oil in Prudhoe Bay. The company was purchased by BP Amoco in 2000.

Aleut - One of three Native Alaskan groups, of the Aleutian Islands

Alyeska - Alyeska Pipeline Service Company

ATCO - ATCO Corporation of Calgary was the company that built the camp barracks.

BP - British Petroleum,the major owner of the pipeline

Bull Cooks - Housekeepers – mostly women. The term comes from the joke that they "couldn't cook a bull."

Cheechako - A person who is a newcomer to Alaska, a tenderfoot. Opposite of sourdough

Drag up - To quit a job for no real reason

Eskimo - Native people who speak Inuit or Yupik. Today, the term Eskimo is little used and is sometimes considered derogatory.

F-27 - A passenger plane or flights to camps

Haul Road - Now called the Dalton Highway

Local 798 - Union Pipeliners (welders), Tulsa, Oklahoma

Mug Up - A room adjacent to the mess hall where coffee and snacks were available 24 hours a day

NANA - NANA Regional Corporation Inc. is one of several Alaska Native corporations. NANA is the parent company of NANA Security.

Parky squirrel - Arctic ground squirrels - They are called "parky squirrels" because their skins are used in traditional clothing – specifically, parkas.

Pipeliners - Union welders of Local 798, Tulsa, Oklahoma

POL -Petroleum/Oil/Lubricants, a place where petroleum products are stored

PS – pump station, see definition below

Pump Station - A permanent pipeline camp and operational facility. During the construction period, there were six pump stations north of the Yukon River (PS-1 - PS-6)

Shoe Pac - A heavy, high-top boot that has rubber soles and leather uppers and a removable felt liner

Sourdough - Original Euro-American settlers and other long-time Alaska residents. Someone who is hardened and accustomed to harsh conditions. Opposite of cheechako.

RCM - Resident Camp Manager

R&R - Rest and relaxation, time off from work

Utilidor - An aboveground, insulated network of pipes and cables, used to convey water and electricity in communities situated in areas of permafrost.

Wackenhut - This company provided security south of Yukon during construction.

Waffle stompers - heavy boots with deep corrugated soles

RELATED READING

Amazing Pipeline Stories: How Building the Trans-Alaska Pipeline Transformed Life in America's Last Frontier, by Dermot Cole, 1997

Crazy Money: Nine Months on the Trans-Alaska Pipeline, by Potter Wickware, 1979

Crude Dreams: A Personal History of Oil & Politics in Alaska, by Jack Roderick, 1997

The Great Alaska Pipeline, by Stan Cohen, 1988

Going to Extremes, by Joe McGinniss, 1980

Inside the Alaska Pipeline, by Ed McGrath, 1977

Journeys Down the Line: Building the Trans-Alaska Pipeline, by Robert Douglas Mead, 1978

800 Miles to Valdez: The Building of the Alaska Pipeline, by James P. Roscow, 1977